Praise for *Common Sense F*
An Atheist's Guide to Alcol

CW01509591

I read the book today and it held me from beginning to end. I like the balanced approach he took and the respectful tone toward our religious friends. I agree with his analogy of religion acting as the ferry that brought us safely to shore. Once ashore, we don't need to get back on the boat, but we don't curse it either. It was truly a nice read and I highly recommend it to all.

John

As someone who has been completely alienated from AA by all the "god talk", it is extremely comforting to confirm that indeed, one does not have to believe in GOD to get, and stay, clean.

Amy

I especially salute how you portray the necessity of us who do not believe to respect those who do. By treating them with respect and dignity, we certainly help ourselves and by extension perhaps them as well.

Thomas B

Read Adam's essays in one sitting. Hard to put into words how amazing they are. Life changing for me. I'm going to print them out, bind it, and use it moving forward in my recovery. Thank you so much!!!

Tiffany O

Non-judgmental and non-confrontational. I love it.

Tommy H

Because I am susceptible to wishful or magical thinking myself, I can empathize with a 1930s collection of recently recovered drunkards that saw their "miracle of sobriety" as God's plan. What's the harm in that? For me however, like Adam, who authored this book, reason is a sounder foundation for me to build a life on today than any kind of supernatural view of the world or recovery.

Joe C

This book gives me hope. It is crisp, concise, easy to read and easy to understand. I found it to be VERY comforting and graciously written. Thank you for writing this book!!

Jean

This is awesome, I wish I had read it sooner. THIS should be what everyone reads when they enter AA regardless of religious belief. This "is" what AA needs to publish.

Michelle

Adam's book is important because it integrates atheism and AA's principles. Many cannot use AA's powerful tools because of the religious language of its literature and of many of its members. Adam assumes that AA's underlying principles work. He accepts them, but understands and explains them "devoid of theistic interpretation". For those of us who are atheists and who also want to use AA to achieve and maintain sobriety, Adam's clarity is a great help.

David R

Start this book and you may consume it in one sitting. Or you can digest it in smaller bites. Either way, you'll return to it. Whether we are new or old to AA, it offers proof that we all belong and can remain, in our own good standing, whether we believe, do not believe, or refuse to enter the argument. And it does so without a lecture. And no yelling.

Dan

Smart and unpretentious. Beautiful.

Dave

COMMON SENSE RECOVERY:

AN ATHEIST'S GUIDE TO ALCOHOLICS ANONYMOUS

THIRD EDITION

BY ADAM N.

Common Sense Recovery:

An Atheist's Guide to Alcoholics Anonymous

Third Edition

N., Adam, 1958-, author

Common Sense Recovery : An Atheist's Guide to Alcoholics
Anonymous / by Adam N. -- Third edition.

First and second editions published by AA Agnostica (2015)

Issued in print and kindle formats:

ISBN: 978-1-0827122-0-3 (pbk.)

ASIN: B07VRSDKXV (kindle)

1. Alcoholics Anonymous. 2. Recovering alcoholics--Religious life.
3. Atheists. I. Title.

Cover design by Carl Rohrs

Interior layout and eBook version formatted by Chris G. (2nd
edition) and Laura L. (3rd edition)

Table of Contents

Acknowledgments

Note for the third edition: Many thanks to AA Agnostica, Roger C., and Chris G. for publishing the first and second editions of *Common Sense Recovery*. Roger saw something he felt would be helpful in my writings, and Chris helped make it all look right so it could be published. I am forever grateful for the opportunity to get my writings out there where they can perhaps be of help to those atheists, agnostics, and freethinkers in AA.

I would like to thank my Mama Teddy for leading the way, both into recovery and into free thinking;

My sister Amy for sharing the long and winding path, always encouraging me to write;

My good friend and great sponsor David R.;

Santa Cruz AA, where my atheism and free thinking are more tolerated than might be in other parts of our world;

And, most of all, to the love of my life Laura Joy for modeling coming out atheist, and for unparalleled, unconditional love, compassion, support, and friendship.

Foreword
By Ward Ewing

From the beginning there has been tension around theism in AA. The connection with the Oxford Group movement meant that, in Akron, a more traditional understanding of God would infuse the emerging fellowship of alcoholics and the book Alcoholics Anonymous. However, in New York, as the Big Book was being written, members expunged any theological positions and expanded the concept of God to "a power greater than ourselves" and to "God as we understood Him." In addition, although the Big Book does not discuss AA groups directly, the use of the plural first person in the Steps and elsewhere indicates this dependence is also on other alcoholics with whom the alcoholic can identify.

Less than ten years later, as Bill W. was developing the Traditions, the ground for this position was made clear: There is only one requirement for membership – the desire to stop drinking. The only authority within an AA group is the group conscience. For the survival of the Fellowship unity is critical, and that unity is found not in agreement but in the primary purpose of living sober and helping the alcoholic. In my personal experience, the Fellowship of Alcoholics Anonymous is, as a result of these principles, the most inclusive organization with which I have been privileged to be associated.

As Bill W. wrote in the Grapevine in July 1965:

> *Newcomers are approaching AA at the rate of tens of thousands yearly. They represent almost every belief and attitude imaginable. We have atheists and agnostics. We*

have people of nearly every race, culture and religion. In AA we are supposed to be bound together in the kinship of a common suffering. Consequently, the full individual liberty to practice any creed or principle or therapy whatever should be a first consideration for us all. Let us not, therefore, pressure anyone with our individual or even our collective views. Let us instead accord each other the respect and love that is due to every human being as he tries to make his way toward the light. Let us always try to be inclusive rather than exclusive; let us remember that each alcoholic among us is a member of AA, so long as he or she declares.

Despite these important points made by Bill W. almost 50 years ago, the tension remains. Recently I was privileged to participate in the first international conference of atheists, agnostics, and free-thinkers in AA. Clearly, many in AA who are atheists, agnostics, and free-thinkers feel excluded. Much of the language in the Big Book, in other approved literature, and in meetings is traditional theistic language. Certain parts of AA literature are at best condescending towards atheists and agnostics, if not downright disparaging, such as the remark in Dr. Bob's story describing atheism, agnosticism, or skepticism as "intellectual pride which keeps [one] from accepting what is in this book."

Admittedly the Big Book, including Dr. Bob's story, was published in 1939 and reflects the earliest experience of AA whereas Bill W.'s statement in the Grapevine exhibits a view based on thirty years experience. Bill's statement may well have been stimulated by his correspondence with Denys W., a self-defined "scientific humanist" from Cambridge, England, who sought to re-think the Big Book and revise the Twelve

Steps to make them more acceptable to committed humanists. (Ernest Kurtz, Not-God, pp. 232-233)

Still, tensions continue in the Fellowship, largely as a result of members who believe the way they found sobriety is the best way. Many who have found sobriety through belief in a traditional theistic God search the Big Book for references that support their contention that their way is the "true way" and they seek to "restore" AA to conform to their understanding. Others, who would focus on the inclusive character of the Fellowship, including the absence of any religious or theological positions, often do the same. Should these tensions tear the Fellowship into hostile camps, the damage to AA would be severe, the ability to carry the message of hope to those who still suffer would be impaired, and the program would be diminished by the loss of the experience of a particular group.

The program of Alcoholics Anonymous developed in a pragmatic manner, based on the experience of members. The primary criterion seems to be "it works". The heart of AA is the sharing of stories, of personal experience – the experience of limitation, that one is unable to control his or her drinking, that one cannot control life or the lives of others, and that seeking such control actually makes life unmanageable. They are stories of letting go of all that baggage and accepting a new way of living that is directed by a power outside the self, a power known primarily through the esprit de corps of the group. Some interpret this transformation as guided by God, as traditionally understood. Yet others see it as the result of "peer support, empathy, mentor guidance, and emotional reinforcement of group membership".

I believe the health and future of AA requires this tension. We are dramatically different people. We have different experiences. We share different stories, seeking to be as honest as possible. The quality of this pragmatic program of recovery depends on the honest sharing by differing people of different experiences. I attend only open meetings and most of them are speaker meetings. What I experience in these meetings is honest disclosure – honest disclosure about drinking and about how the Fellowship has worked for the speaker. When I attend open discussion meetings, I am always impressed by the lack of cross talk and by the intense level of listening. I've come to understand that listening is one of the keys to recovery. We listen to hear truth – not dogmatic, theological, mathematical, or philosophical truths, but personal truth about feelings, faults, sneaky motivations – fearless honesty. "Identify, don't compare" you tell me. Experience is the key. From such honest sharing comes the support that makes the impossible possible.

Adam N. has written an important book, sharing his experience as an atheist in the Fellowship, an experience that included dropping out of AA after twenty years of sobriety. As he describes what happened, "I grew restless, irritable, and malcontent. I heard nothing new, had heard it all before, and was totally over it. Meetings just felt like a waste of my valuable time. The slogans ceased to be wise aphorisms and morphed into moronic truisms." For him AA had come to feel like a religious cult for "the simple minded" based on "mindless dogma" and accepting "fairy tales as profound truths." He had come to find honest sharing of his doubts, his unorthodox, science-friendly free thinking, to be alienating, and that became a major factor in his leaving AA. Three years without AA and a "torturous year and a half of active alcohol and narcotics addiction" led to a return to treatment and AA. As he re-entered the Fellowship, he recognized that previously he "had held something in reserve all along. I am, when all is said and done, an atheist." Fearless honesty – necessary for continued sobriety –led him to write this book with the hope of clarifying for himself how to interpret the religiously laden language of AA. This book has been published in the hopes that it might serve to widen the doors for others who suffer from this cunning, baffling, and powerful disease, whether they be theists, atheists, agnostics, free-thinkers, skeptics, or secularists.

What I like best about this book is its focus on experience. The narrative is essentially one drunk sharing his story with others who may be helped by that sharing. The heart of AA is the sharing of one's story, of one's experience. Adam's journey is one of seeking fearless honesty and a deeper understanding of the dynamics of the AA Fellowship. In the end, I interpret him as moving to a new kind of faith. This faith is not in some unseen magical being but is in the program and fellowship of Alcoholics Anonymous. This is a faith based not on doctrinal (or Big Book) correctness or some theoretical belief, but a faith based on experience, a faith that is pragmatic, free of religion, transformational, and focused on concern for others. In the program of Alcoholics Anonymous, which developed over the years in a pragmatic manner based on the experience of members, his sharing represents the mainstream, even if it is not often heard. This is an expression of his experience, and we can identify with him if we look for the similarities rather than differences.

While this essay is written primarily for the atheist, agnostic, and free thinker in AA, I encourage those who see themselves as religious to read it as well. I have many reasons. First and foremost Adam is sharing his story. That sharing is the foundation of Alcoholics Anonymous. This is the language of the heart; all need to listen respectfully, with an openness to learn. Second, many who claim to be religious worship a god that is too small, a god who seems to be a personal servant. We must listen to the critiques of belief and current religious practice. They provide an opportunity for growth and maturity. And finally, religious members should read this book in the name of all inclusiveness. In keeping with the third tradition, every member of Alcoholics Anonymous can benefit from becoming sensitized to concerns about excluding members and potential members. In the name of the unity of this Fellowship we must all be committed to affirm that there is common ground for all members of this Fellowship, be they theistic, agnostic, atheistic or whatever.

Adam speaks of "immersion in [a] fellowship [that] offers us exactly the life sustaining support we need, feeding us at a core level, bringing us an increased sense of personal value, purpose, emotional fulfillment and peace of mind." The power of AA is greater than any individual person; it makes the impossible possible. Many in AA refer to this lifesaving force, this culture, this esprit de corps, this higher power, as God. Others who cannot bring themselves to compromise their rational understandings, to believe in some sort of deity, still experience this power within AA groups. I would suggest that the differences between those who wish to call it God and those who have a different understanding of its nature are small in comparison to our shared experience. What we believe about something is far less important to living than what we experience. Experience is what transforms us; belief is our attempt to explain. Experience trumps explanation. Experience provides the basis for the dialogue between those who are religious and those who are free thinkers, agnostics, and atheists in AA. I thank Adam for sharing his experience. I hope it will be a means for strengthening the unity of the AA Fellowship, as AA is all about supporting each other in recovery and in carrying the message – regardless of belief or lack of belief.

Ward B. Ewing

Retired Dean and President of the General Theological Seminary

Trustee emeritus (non-alcoholic) and past Chair of the General Service Board

Preface

Sometimes I feel like a spy. It can be very exciting, kind of thrilling. I've enjoyed spy novels, seen the movies.

But sometimes it makes me feel alone, isolated. Unseen. Unheard.

I am a member of two sub-cultures within the broader American culture. Unfortunately, these two sub-cultures within which I currently dwell tend to be in direct opposition. First and foremost, I am a recovering alcoholic. Like so many of my kind, I have found freedom from my addiction to alcohol and other drugs through the sub-culture we call Alcoholics Anonymous. This culture has strong roots in christian tradition, and places a heavy emphasis upon religious beliefs.

Therein lays the tension. For decades I have worked very hard, with an emphasis on the latter half of the third step, to get comfortable with some form of religious or spiritual way of seeing things. Try as I might, I could not succeed. In the end, I have found great peace of mind and happiness through being true to myself and accepting that I am an atheist. That is, I do not believe in God, or gods, or anything supernatural, and avoid like the plague the usage of vague and meaningless terms like god, spirit, spiritual, or usually even higher power. This places me in a sub-culture within a sub-culture: the atheist in Alcoholics Anonymous. So, I am like a double agent.

For years now I have had to play the role of the interpreter. I take the religious ideas and language of AA and translate it into atheistic language, language to which I can relate and which means something to me. I am the atheist embedded. I am surrounded by people who speak a foreign language and who might be vaguely, if not overtly, hostile were they to know my true thoughts.

Yet I also find that I am often more tolerant of religious thinking than many of my atheistic brethren. For one, I have studied and tried to walk the "spiritual" path, and have some empathy for their struggles and their perspectives. For another, I am sensitive to the fact that many of the life saving principles embodied in the twelve step recovery programs are borrowed or developed from religious sources. I have a great deal of respect for that. I do not hate religion per se. I just think it is outdated. It is time for us to move on, grow up. It is a very exciting time to be alive. I say that as a lover of science and scientific discovery, as an atheist and a lover of truth, and as the fortunate recipient of all the community building which modern technology enables and encourages. A very exciting time indeed.

So, one day I set out to clarify for myself exactly what the religiously laden language spoken within the rooms of AA meant to me, to translate it into a-theistic, humanist terms. That is what this work was initially all about. I sought primarily to clarify the core, operative principles which saved us all and kept us living, and to divorce them from the obfuscating religious language. Thus clarified, I could sit in meetings or read "approved" literature without getting ticked off, sidetracked by confusion, irritated, frustrated or resentful. I could just calmly translate the spiritualese into humanese, and get on with my own recovery. Writing this work helped strengthen me in terms of my sobriety, and my atheism as well.

I figured to write in obscurity until the worms ate me. Much to my surprise, it appears I am bound for some degree of exposure whilst still upright and ambulatory. This is perfect.

Having just read *Coming Out Atheist*, I have been convinced by its author, Greta Christina, that we atheists have a moral obligation to come out of the closet. This is especially true for those of us within the twelve step sub-culture. I genuinely believe that lives depend upon it, and that we are practicing the twelfth step when, as atheists, we challenge the status quo and, if only slightly, widen the doors of AA to those who may feel excluded or put off by the religious emphasis, but who still suffer from active addiction and alcoholism. So, as frightening as going public may be, I do so enthusiastically, with two heartfelt hopes.

My first hope is that my thoughts might be helpful to fellow atheists, agnostics and free thinkers in recovery as they make their way along their own path, just as the shared thoughts and experiences of so many others have been of help to me. I hope that my words might serve to strengthen them as they walk the fine line between these two important realities, reaffirming the fact that they are not alone.

My second hope is that my writing might stimulate ongoing dialogue on these topics which are so dear to me, and that I might have the opportunity to participate in that dialogue and whatever changes may begin to ensue. If you would like to engage in dialogue about the views presented in this book, I highly suggest a visit to one of the following websites: AA Beyond Belief or AA Agnostica.

My Life in a Few Pages

My name is Adam. I am an alcoholic and a drug addict. I opened my first bar when I was 9 years old. It was constructed from Drambuie liqueur boxes and had "Adam's Bar" colorfully spray painted across the front. With my parent's blessings, a noteworthy hint of pride in fact, I mixed their Gin and Tonics, Rum and Cokes, Martini's to order, the whole shebang. Eventually I earned underground notoriety as the only bar in the U.S. Virgin Islands open on Good Friday.

When I later took to my own serious drinking, I never looked back. I'd never felt so much freedom from fear, self-consciousness, and anxiety. I had never felt so good about myself, never fit in so well. I became a full-time consumer, an alcoholic, mid-level, drug-dealing teen in New York City's Central Park. Progression ensued, my dreams and ambitions and curiosity and motivation all washed away in an ever deepening sea of Jack Daniels, Rolling Rock and Heineken. The slide was greased with daily marijuana, occasional serious hallucinogens, and an on-again-off-again furious obsession with cocaine. I escaped New York City just as heroin started to become the fad amongst my peers, later to find that it cut a wide swath of death and destruction through my posse of friends and acquaintances.

I was shipped by my loving family off to the sunny left coast, where I was supposed to continue my schooling. There, unsurprisingly, unoriginally, I majored in sex, drugs, and rock-n-roll. In these, I excelled. Unfortunately, the University of California failed to recognize my genius in these fields as academically pertinent.

The inevitable bottom approached and, with everything falling apart and a rapidly expanding emptiness inside me, I was ready for change. It was at this point that I began to become consciously aware of personal "powerlessness" at its most devastating. Having seriously made up my mind to change, I found myself entirely unable to do so. Every attempt to stop or moderate failed miserably.

I cried to my Mommy and Daddy. Within a week I was on a plane, drinking those two or three sad, pointless, "goodbye" beers, on my way to the deep frozen tundra of December Minnesota to the adolescent treatment ward at Hazelden.

My sober life began there, a new and entirely different life, with Alcoholics Anonymous at its core. Everything started to change. The boy who had been unable to go hours without a drink or a drug was OK with being completely clean and sober for days, weeks, months, years. The unemployed and unemployable juvenile delinquent became an excellent employee, quickly rising to trusted positions in management. No longer was I a constant drain on friends and family, a source of worry, someone to be avoided. Instead I became a loved, welcomed, useful member of family and society. The woman who had dumped me now married me. The angry, grungy boy who had scowled and spat at staring children on the streets of New York City now stayed at home to nurture and love three of his own, chasing them giggling around playgrounds, teaching them how to garden, dancing and singing with purple dinosaurs on TV, curling up and reading them bedtime stories at night. Neighborhood mothers entrusted him with their own little angels. From academic probation to Highest Honors; from cheater and philanderer to stable, reliable husband; from untrustworthy drunkard to good, trustworthy man.

This is a true story. This amazing transformation was entirely true and real, and entirely the effect of Alcoholics

Anonymous in my life. Even more remarkable is the fact that, in AA, these stories are not so much remarkable as fairly common place.

But after twenty years of this good life, I grew tired of AA. I grew restless, irritable, and malcontent. I heard nothing new, had heard it all before, and was totally over it. Meetings just felt like a waste of my valuable time. The slogans ceased to be wise aphorisms and morphed into moronic truisms. Long lingering reservations began to blossom. AA felt more and more like a cult of the simple-minded, shot through with an unspoken hive agreement to genially submit to mindless dogma, to willingly accept fairy tales as profound truths.

I had struggled with and tolerated and attempted to translate the religious language into something I could relate to for half my adult life. But the distance grew and grew. Alcoholics Anonymous, with its god-this and spirit-that, came to feel more like an unnecessary burden than a life saving necessity. I ceased to relate, dissecting and critically analyzing my way right out of the life raft that had saved me from certain death.

At first, rationalizations worked fine. I was in service to others, caring for kids and family all day long. The teachings of AA were, in fact, deeply embedded in me. I remained clean and sober for three years with no meetings, no sponsors, no Big Book, and no real work with other alcoholics. But slowly, imperceptibly, I began to change. Self pity, depression, anger and cynicism began to dominate my life. I was a sitting duck. With no defense against that first drink or drug, it was only a matter of time before something happened. And then something happened.

What followed was a torturous year and a half of active alcohol and narcotics addiction. Bad for me. Maybe even worse for my loving sister and family, for my wife, who had known only a sober husband for our entire marriage, and for our three teenage children, who had never known their father to take a single drink, much less be a stumbling, nodding, slurring, embarrassing drunkard.

Newfound levels of despair and hopelessness coupled with the familiar misery of old. I dragged my embarrassed, prideful ass back into AA on numerous occasions. From respected old timer to pathetic newcomer-the shame was beyond description. But the disease was too strong. Once again I faced the reality of my own powerlessness. I could not stop. I'd stay sober days, weeks, even months, but eventually succumb to the lies screaming in my head, drowning out the "program's" teachings. The overwhelming demons could only be quieted by my concession to their destructive commands. Once again I'd enjoin the futile pursuit of chemical well-being, chasing the happiness I imagined was only available in pill and powder, herb and bottle.

The experience was positively medieval. I could almost see the demons that owned me, each day growing stronger, louder, larger. Meanwhile the angels who had guided me for so long grew smaller, weaker, receded cowering into the shadows. Overpowering obsession coupled with an unending justificatory monologue in my head, literally forcing me to drink. I could not stop. I was powerless.

Finally, I surrendered myself to a local treatment facility, locked down for 28 days away from temptation, in order to break the cycle. There I re-awakened and began once again to employ the principles of recovery that had guided me for so much of my life. I reentered AA once again, deep into middle age, a newcomer yet an old timer, yet neither. I came back with the best attitude an arrogant, over-educated, self-loathing narcissist could muster. Repetition was fine. Simple slogans were fine. Religious dogma was fine. Whatever you told me to do, I'd do. I worked the steps again, surrender and self-reflection and confession and restitution.

But, while my two decades and more of sobriety had been filled with excellence and goodness, I believe I had held something in reserve all along. I am, when all is said and done, an atheist. Once again god, spirituality and religion were front and center in my life, screaming at me from every page in the Big Book. This time around I fully awakened to the fact that, in spite of decades of effort to change, I was, in my heart of hearts, a non-believer.

This struggle to be something I was not was at the heart of my relapse. I mouthed the religious language of AA, I talked the talk. But at a very basic, core level, I was never able to buy it hook, line, and sinker.

The Atheist Embedded

Like it or not, the religious viewpoint predominates in Alcoholics Anonymous. An honest reading of the primary text is enough to convince anyone. The chapter entitled "We Agnostics", for example, is not a welcome embrace so much as a sales pitch intended to draw non-believers gently into the fold, towards the inevitable end of their being convinced. The stated goal of the book is to guide us toward the kind of spiritual awakening which will solve our drink problem and put us on a better path. From the point of view of the more devout religious members, this means to get us to god consciousness.

Hard as it might be to tell based solely upon my arrogant, atheistic ranting, I have seriously tried throughout my life to put on religious garb. Fascinating fact #1: approximately 90% of persons on the planet grow up to hold the religious beliefs of their family or primary culture. I am, in a way, no exception. I was raised by two rather virulently anti-theistic parents. The exploratory and rebellious teenage years found me rebelling not against religion, but rather against atheism.

Unlike my entire family, I opened my mind to religious insights. Fueled somewhat by the sub-culture of druggies within which I spent much of my teen youth, I experimented and studied, cranking out papers on eastern religious philosophy. I was courted by department heads to join their religious studies programs. All of which is to say that I had an uncharacteristically open mind on the subject. I immersed myself in the works of Alan Watts and Krishnamurti. I am not sure if it was my daily consumption of chemical cocktails or my religious leanings which more worried my neo-Bohemian, east coast liberal, atheistic parents. My point here is to let the reader know that I have, from an early age, been very much of the open-minded school, and have been quick to see where the religious people are right throughout most of my life.

Eventually, I stumbled desperately into Alcoholics Anonymous. It was 1983, and I was in my mid-20s. I came under the wing of some well-meaning, but rather serious, old time Big Book thumpers. These were the kind of guys who had known Bill and Bob personally. I bought their hard line, that if you don't do it exactly as it is written and as we old timers insist, you will not survive. As a consequence I have strived with extreme due diligence to do it that way.

For years I bought what I now call the "Bill" view: the good is the enemy of the best. In a nutshell, perfectionism combined with old-school dogmatism. I have subsequently, after decades of trial, success, and error, switched to a more compassionate and tolerant view, one which is more in line with Bob's assertion that, "if we go about this thing with half the zeal we showed in finding our next drink, we'll be alright".

But, before getting to this more tolerant, diversity-embracing perspective, I was still under the sway of the hardliners. During that time I lived and worked all twelve steps, numerous times, reciting the various step-prayers associated with them for decades; going to numerous Catholic retreats; joining Unitarian churches; studying Buddhist belief, behavior, written word and visual art; practicing yoga and meditation; reading Aquinas and Anselm, Tillich, Buber, Thich Nhat Hanh and many more; studiously immersing myself in every drop of approved AA literature and recovery-oriented self-help works, from Emmet Fox to *The Road Less Traveled*, that I could get my hands on; practicing daily prayer and meditation; praying to icons of Sakyamuni and Maitreya, Saint Francis,

Jesus Christ, the Christian cross, the giant redwoods, the ocean, door knobs, and, perhaps most importantly, the ever-infamous Porcelain God. You name it, I've tried it.

In spite of my very best efforts, I am unable to be convinced of god, spirit or soul. Perhaps that formative first decade of life, being raised from birth in an entirely atheistic environment, was definitive. But, fortunately, I am in good company. Many excellent and devout persons, from Milarepa to Muhammad to Mother Theresa, have grappled with faith, have struggled with doubt. Many good and wise people have also given up the struggle, have contentedly embraced life as non-theists. What I am proposing is the unconditional acceptance of this latter alternative. This is the viewpoint with which I am most comfortable, which seems right to me. Belief in god is not necessary for recovery from alcoholism or addiction. It is optional only. Further, it may, in fact, be detrimental in the long run.

Don't get me wrong: I love Alcoholics Anonymous. I truly believe it is the best game in town, as far as beating alcoholism and drug addiction is concerned. Today I am a grateful, active and involved participant, having attended AA meetings for over half my life. Yet, I have always grappled with the religious components of AA. At best it's been "fake it till you make it".

I have been able to achieve lasting sobriety through AA. But I have had to do a lot of reading between the lines along the way. I've had to make sense of religious language. Like a spy forced to remain in a foreign land, I've had to learn the interpretive skills necessary to survive, to understand their experience in light of my own. I've become adept at translating what is said so that it makes sense from a humanistic, secular and scientific point of view.

The following is a series of reflections based upon my years of experience as an atheist embedded in Alcoholics Anonymous. My claim is that god is optional, not required, for a successful recovery program. But you will get seriously chewed out by some well meaning, protective old timers if you talk like this at an AA meeting. The fact that the thoughts that I am articulating here would be considered blasphemous if spoken aloud at a meeting, well, that's why I'm writing this book. My hope is to see atheism normalized within the recovery community.

Atheism should not be stigmatized. We should not have to hide our beliefs, to "come out of the closet" and risk being ostracized. But the truth is that atheism is mostly just tolerated. The most common response we encounter is a charitable smirk implying that, if we come around long enough, we will eventually "come to", and then, inevitably, if we are doing it right, we will "come to believe" more less as the other theists do.

A further point worth considering, however, is whether we might be more effectively of service, reach more suffering alcoholics. We might save more lives. There may be millions of alcoholics and addicts out there suffering and dying while we sit comfortably in the rooms of AA proclaiming its effectiveness.

I will not cite the various studies which have thrown this confidence into doubt. The reader can easily find them for him or herself. Suffice to say that, as a matter of fact, the number of alcoholics who come to AA and remain long term is much smaller than the number of potential members who stay away from AA altogether, or who come to AA and don't "get it". If we truly care about the alcoholics who still suffer, if we truly wish to be of service to others, we have an obligation to be open-minded about exactly what message we are carrying, its effectiveness and accessibility.

I firmly believe that, while the religious emphasis may indeed be beneficial for some, it sends away at least as many as it saves. Many of these go on to suffer the horrid fate, the "hell" if you like, that only addicts and alcoholics can know. We sober members remain in the rooms, patting each others' backs, consoling ourselves with the thought that the man or woman will return "when they are ready". "If the god thing scares them away, alcohol will beat them back", we like to say.

We also like to say "If it ain't broke, don't fix it". But don't such self-congratulatory recitations merely serve to salve our feelings, consoling those few of us who do "get it" so that we do not have to face the hard, stark possibility that recovery methodology might be made roomier, more all inclusive?

If god is truly optional, we may be unnecessarily turning away people who need and want what we have. We then compound this sin by consoling ourselves with the *a posteriori* rationalization that "they weren't ready yet".

As recovering alcoholics, certainly we are familiar with this process of erring, then subsequently rationalizing our behavior. This was a primary modus operandi for us for years, and we all know it did not automatically cease when we put the plug in the jug. Are we, as a group, guilty of the same kind of self-justification when we put mystical belief systems and faith healing at the core of our project and then blame the non-believers who walk out, or never walk in the first place??

In spite of my ego, I am not one to say that all this talk about god, religion or spirituality is right or wrong. What the hell do I know, really? I am simply sharing my experience, as a believer in reason and as a non-theist, in my efforts to make sense of and employ the main concepts and practices. I write this essay as a project to help me get clear on all of this for myself, to come to terms with the gap. But, as I write, I gain hope that others will be aided by this interpretive narrative, that these kinds of thoughts might make the contemporary recovery methodology more accessible to those who are similarly unable to buy the religious slant of Alcoholics Anonymous.

Spiritual Caulk and the Great Puppeteer in the Sky

One of the most profound insights I've discovered in atheist literature is that god concepts serve the purpose of filling in gaps in our knowledge. "Miracles" like lightening and earthquakes and sudden changes in personalities were considered inexplicable. In order to satisfy the natural human hunger for explanation deities were invoked. To this day god serves the same purpose. Simply put, when we do not understand how something works, we chalk it up to god. God serves as a metaphysical caulk, a generic, all-purpose filler that effectively fills in the gaps in our understanding.

One time at an AA meeting at San Francisco's 1010 Valencia I heard a woman talk about a ride on a city bus. She was fairly new to sobriety, feeling pretty shaky at the time. As she rode the city bus she looked up and, there on the seat directly before her, she recognized a fellow member of AA. This chance encounter and their subsequent interaction helped her through a difficult time. She interpreted this as a miracle. She described it as "god working in her life", a very common expression in the rooms of AA.

This is what I have come to refer to, yes, somewhat derisively I confess, as the puppeteer god. It refers to the idea that god arranges worldly matters to reinforce our AA lifestyle, to miraculously guide our "spiritual" development. This god is very helpful, offers us numerous opportunities for growth, but never gives us more than we can handle. On good days god even finds us parking places when we are on the verge of being late for some important event, like an AA meeting or a job interview. The puppeteer also likes to miraculously inspire our sponsor to call us just when we most need to hear from him or her. I understand the comfort such beliefs bring. A safe, orderly world. Like a household in which a caring, attentive parent oversees all.

But I wondered as she spoke, hadn't this other fellow been on that bus before? Undoubtedly when she was still "in her cups", that same rider was right there, sitting before her unnoticed. In fact that very same rider might have been sitting across the way, waving a Big Book directly in her face just the day before. But she would have been unable to acknowledge this fortuitous encounter and all the mutual good that it afforded. Perhaps she had been blinded to the world around her as she obsessed over how and where she was going to get her next fix, pill or drink.

Wasn't the difference, the real deal maker in this scenario, our speaker's newfound willingness to perceive and imbue with value this most excellent opportunity for enhancing her recovery? Wasn't her newfound openness and willingness really the crux of the matter, regardless of theistic interpretations?

I find it very difficult to relate to the sharing of AA members whose Higher Power arranges the world to fix them. They utilize god to fill in the void in their understanding when interesting and impressive things happen in their lives. To me this just smacks of mental laziness. I feel very uncomfortable in meetings where this sort of thing takes place. I think they are dismissing the power of genuine willingness in their lives, denigrating the incredible capacity of humans to embrace change and transform for the better.

If you choose to interpret recovery experiences in this way, you are left with some inexplicable and particularly onerous implications. For example, why did god not similarly come to the rescue of Freddy, or Jim, or Alice, or Tom? Each of them has relapsed and are now out stumbling drunk or shooting up in an alley somewhere. Why did the puppeteer not come to their aid? Is there a merit system involved? Is it karma? Unlikely to be the case, as we all know miscreants who have been spared, yet sweethearts who have succumbed.

I believe that the real work in our bus rider's life is being done largely by her newfound attitude. She is open to solutions and opportunities to grow her recovery that, prior to this time, she could not even have recognized. She is ready for new, life changing experiences that could move her forever away from the needle and the bottle, and instead towards sober well-being. This mindset, of open-mindedness and willingness, is essential to recovery. Theistic interpretations are not. And it is this newfound mindset that's really doing the heavy lifting here. Not god.

Courage to Change

Prayer and meditation are among the most obvious examples of definitively religious practices considered essential to recovery. This morning, ironic though it may be, I prayed before returning to these blasphemous writings. Why? Because I need a daily restoration to sanity and this activity is a learned and habitual component in that process.

But the heavy lifting in prayer is not done by anything outside of us. The puppeteer deity does not meet our requests, or deny them, or even hear them. Through prayer and meditation we make fundamental changes to ourselves. It is an act of commitment and recommitment to a new set of values. But there is nothing that is literally miraculous involved, no outside deity at work. Praying for people, places and things does nothing to affect the people, places or things in question. What it can do is change us, and thereby our relationships with the people, places and things in question. What prayer does is simply change our thinking, our emotions, our action choices, and thereby everything about our relationships with the rest of the world.

AA members often jest that we should be careful what we ask for. A common interpretation is that, when you begin to pray for something, to ask god for something, god will present you with opportunities to develop or earn that thing. Say, for example, you discover in your inventory process you suffer from impatience. Recognizing this as a defect in your character, you subsequently pray for increased patience.

The popular mythology in AA is that, at this point, The Great Puppeteer in the Sky will place before you a frustrating series of circumstances intended to shine a spotlight on your impatience. "Our higher power presents us with opportunities for growth." Having become ready to have this defect removed, god now tests, or forges, us through exposure to temptation. That god gives us what we need in order to allow us the opportunity to develop our character is a historically common theistic interpretation.

But it is fairly easy to see how a non-believer, or conversely, if you will, one who believes in human potential, can interpret such experiences as simply highlighting our newfound sensitivity and awareness, along with our newfound willingness to change. Occam's Razor, or the Law of Parsimony, suggests that, all other things being equal, we should employ the explanation which posits the least extra parts, as it were. Certainly employing supernatural deities to explain straightforward psychological and social phenomenon directly conflicts with this most common sense philosophical principle.

Consider, for example, the sixth and seventh steps of Alcoholics Anonymous. These prescribe for us that we become willing to have god remove all of our defects of character and humbly ask him to do so. If we work the steps with genuine honesty, open-mindedness and a willingness to change, we will come to identify our negative tendencies and reach a state of willingness to change. From here on out, if we are genuinely interested in changing, we will be hyper-aware of these traits and their consequences in our daily life. This newfound sensitivity to both the trait and its impact on self and society are sufficient, when coupled with an awareness of viable alternatives, to fully explain the process.

This is what happens when we identify problematic tendencies (steps 4 and 5), and subsequently become willing to change (steps 6 and 7). Through this process of honest and critical self-reflection we are now more acutely aware both of the behavioral propensities and of their negative effects upon self and society. We have heightened our awareness and see these things at work in our lives with greater honesty than ever before. Most of us are aware that some practice is then required, as we strive daily to employ different behaviors when the occasion arises to do so. In this manner we slowly but surely change our habits of word and deed regarding the problematic behavior.

An introduction to viable alternative attitudes and actions

+

A genuine willingness to change

+

The passage of time

=

All the defect removal we need.

The result of this process is that we can be significantly transformed. Some defects are removed quickly and easily, perhaps because they are directly correlated with using behaviors. These fall to the wayside as physical sobriety begins. But many defects of character we must grapple with slowly over time. Willingness to change includes being honest enough to identify the defects, to face their effects on ourselves and those around us, to see the daily flare-ups, to learn alternative attitudes and actions from our fellowship or literature, and then to practice the implementation of those alternative methods in our daily lives.

On this "one day at a time" basis we experience slow, yet certain, incremental change. We gain nothing by understanding these profound transformations as dependent upon theistic intervention. In fact, we may be inclined to take less responsibility, to wait for the miracle rather than work for the change.

Sometimes a genuine spirit of willingness will create moments of inspiration, moments of sudden change. This, too, should come as no surprise. These rapid changes are miraculous, indeed, in the sense that they are often life-changing and profound. But whether the change is slow and incremental or sudden and immediate neither requires theistic interpretation. In fact, by so doing, we denigrate the amazing and wondrous capacity of humans to change for the better. Perhaps taking the blame for the bad, while giving god credit for the good, is an antiquated and counter-productive tradition.

The changes brought about by a life in AA can indeed seem profound, even miraculous. We are surprised. One day we could think of nothing but alcohol or drugs, and would obsessively, energetically and compulsively shape our lives around the need to use them constantly, regardless of the horrendous damage done to ourselves and to those around us. The next day (seemingly) we are caring, sober, responsible, unselfish and kind people, almost entirely transformed. We do not recognize that there is within us this capacity for transformation which is perfectly and entirely explicable on humanistic grounds. Because the change is beyond our understanding, we apply the spiritual caulk, the fill-all in our understanding that is "god". But the caulk is not needed. Miracles happen every day. I know. I am one of them. If you are reading this, you are probably one too. But god is not required to make sense of them. In fact, in so doing, we denigrate and belittle our own innate capacity for transformation and positive change.

Straight from the Book

In the beginning, there were twelve steps…

No, wait, was that ten? Or were there six?

In the eighth story of the 4th edition of the book *Alcoholics Anonymous*, titled "He Sold Himself Short", the author enumerates the "Six-Step program" of recovery (p. 263). This describes what our founders did to get and stay well. Much of this was gleaned from the Oxford Groups. The allegedly divinely inspired twelve steps were in fact no more than an elaboration on these six fundamental principles. They were not handed down from god, but were simply the result of human reflection and the distilled experience (pun intended) of a bunch of sobered up drunks.

The six fundamental principles of recovery described were:

1. Complete deflation

2. Dependence and guidance from a Higher Power

3. Moral Inventory

4. Confession

5. Restitution

6. Continued work with other alcoholics

These describe actions and attitudes which have been essential to my enjoying a sustainable, useful, and contented sobriety. Their importance cannot be overstated. The emphasis upon religion, on the contrary, can be, and generally is, overstated. The most interesting thing about this list is the absence of a strictly religious emphasis. Higher power is mentioned once. In my view this is easily reconcilable with a secular view, as we learn to depend upon and accept guidance from our fellow AAs, sponsors, and the wisdom of the larger fellowship as a whole. On the other hand, God, higher power, "Him" and spiritual awakening are specified ten times in the current popular form of twelve steps as popularized by Bill Wilson and AA.

Also from the book…

Towards the end of the chapter titled "Into Action" we find some more important new actions and attitudes. Paragraphs beginning with "On awakening…", "As we go through the day…", and "When we retire at night…" offer up very specific, applicable reminders, gleaned from our collective experience, of how we might handle life better than we had prior to getting sober.

For example, upon awakening we are to ask that our thinking be "divorced from self-pity, dishonest or self seeking motives." (p. 86) Since being introduced to this practice I have regularly done this, but again suggest that maybe my willingness to consistently cultivate and affirm these laudable standards is the active ingredient. Prayer serves as a deep reminder and affirmation of such newfound values. I need to re-commit to these on a regular basis, often multiple times a day. Similarly, I need to "pause, when agitated or doubtful", (p. 87) cultivating a mental state of surrender and acceptance, in order to avoid acting upon selfish, fearful or otherwise destructive impulses.

This one small section of the Big Book lays out some profoundly valuable and immanently practical advice for us. When we live this way, we are very different people with very different lives. How many active addicts go to bed constructively reviewing their day to determine where they had been "resentful, selfish, dishonest or afraid" in order to repair the damage and do differently next time? (p. 86)

I distinctly recall maudlin tears and pitiful sobbing pleas for forgiveness, but nothing even remotely resembling a calm moment of prudent self reflection. Being a hard-core blackout drinker, I had many mornings when I came to with absolutely no recollection of the previous night's events. But I would be willing to bet that I had not spent the latter moments of my previous evening "constructively reviewing" my day in any coherent or productive sense.

I read or recall this particular section on an almost daily basis. It is of the utmost importance to my continued recovery, from the way I start my day, through the reminders to pause, to clearing myself of selfish motives, being open to insight and inspiration, all the way to the constructive self reflection when my head hits the pillow at night. Bill W. and the authors of the original text make numerous references to god in these instructional pages. But the important, operative principles, though at one time associated with god, religion or spirituality, are all strong enough to stand on their own. And it is these operative principles, devoid of theistic interpretations, which should be our focus.

Fake It Till You Make It

When I was a fairly young sprite in recovery, with only four or five years clean and sober, my sponsor, known as "Spiritual" Ed, introduced me to the Stag 12 X 12 group. There I found the kind of crusty old timers so definitive of Alcoholics Anonymous. A mere youth in my mid 30s, I found myself surrounded by 50, 60, 70 year old geezers who had been sober as long as I had been alive. And there, hanging on the wall of that hallowed yet dingy meeting hall, I found the following slogan/prayer/saying:

> *We cannot think our way into right living,*

> *But we can live our way into right thinking.*

This simple statement encompasses one of the essential principles of sustained recovery. As irreligious as this may sound, much of recovery simply boils down to behavioral conditioning. We are what we do. The most important way to change character traits is to consistently practice different behaviors. This is true regardless of our mental state. The thoughts and motivations behind our behaviors will follow suit, given time and consistent effort. This is the gist of the common AA expression "Fake it till you make it".

The most obvious example is, of course, that treatment for alcoholism primarily consists of not taking the first drink. If we can do this long enough, the cravings weaken until they are merely thoughts. Then the thoughts, too, weaken, so long as we do not let them build a nest or put down roots. They come with less frequency, with less intensity, until one day we realize that they have been replaced by a new and different set of thoughts, values, beliefs and behaviors. We find that we have recovered from a seemingly hopeless state of mind and body. The drink problem has been solved.

When I have experienced thoughts or cravings, I have been much consoled by the realization that, if I choose not to nurture or act upon the thought or craving, it will begin to diminish in both frequency and intensity. This gives me hope for the future. I guess you could say I believe in this empirical fact, I have faith in this observable, measurable phenomenon. At some point, days, weeks, or months down the road, the haunting demons will wither and atrophy from disuse until they are essentially impotent. And as long as I maintain a lifestyle which encourages continued recovery, they need never again regain their once dominant status.

Now that this fundamental problem has been solved, we alcoholics and addicts are freed, readied and empowered to apply this simple secular recipe for change to all the other areas of our lives. Do the next right thing for long enough and, sure enough, your thoughts, desires and values can all be radically transformed.

Science is Not a Four-Letter Word

A lot has been learned since Bill and Bob first met. I like to think that they did not so much set things in stone as set them in motion.

But we must always keep in our minds that the deep roots of AA in religion have set into our fellowship a long standing tone of anti-science and anti-learning. Religious organizations such as Alcoholics Anonymous tend to be subtly, if not overtly, hostile to new ideas, to science, to change, and to anyone or anything which calls into question their traditional view that the big and important questions have all been answered, and the answer is God.

I am not an expert on the subject matter, and this is not going to be a science paper. Yet we would be doing ourselves and all the suffering alcoholics, now and in the future, in and out of the rooms, a huge disservice if we failed to recognize the ways in which a rapidly expanding body of knowledge might enhance our efforts. So, for example, there is an ever-growing body of scientific data to support the view that positive thinking and associated actions can literally re-wire the brain's circuitry.

So let's consider just one important area of investigation which will suggest the kind of exploration I think we have an obligation to more diligently pursue. Recent findings in the neurosciences suggest that the human brain is more malleable than once thought to be. Our experiences can actually rewire our "plastic" brain. Simply put, when we form habits of behavior, such as drinking or any of the destructive habits of thought associated with the alcoholic lifestyle, we forge strong pathways in our brain, neural connections that are reinforced over and over again, becoming stronger and stronger each time we repeat the patterns of thought and behavior.

The good news is that change is possible. The even better news is that positive change, consistently different thoughts and actions, will re-wire our neural pathways, literally changing our brain's structure. The more we engage in the new behavior, the more that particular set of neurons fires together and wires together. The new connections, perhaps very tenuous at first, grow stronger and stronger with each reinforcing positive thought and activity. Meanwhile, the old pathway literally begins to atrophy from non use. The old habits fade, while the new ones become stronger and stronger with each repetition.

I find it encouraging that we have this growing body of evidence supporting many of our traditional teachings. Repeated alternate behavior choices can actually restructure our mental map. "Fake it till you make it" is scientifically verifiable. "Living our way into right thinking" is not a mere slogan on the wall, but an empirically verifiable technique for altering our brain chemistry and, thereby, our entire lives. How encouraging to know that, as hard as it may be at first to have an "attitude of gratitude", habitually cultivating one through practice and repetition can, over time, literally change the way we see the world at the most basic level.

One of the more influential books I have ever read in my own personal recovery is an old school classic called *A New Pair of Glasses*, by Chuck C. Amongst many other insights, the book offered up the idea that god was in fact, simply, a new way of seeing the world, a new pair of glasses. This idea is suggested throughout the Big Book. The whole point of the AA experience is to initiate a "psychic change" (p. xxix), one which will "revolutionize our whole attitude toward life" and "toward our fellows". (p. 25. Here, as in many places, I intentionally edit out Bill and the old timers' copious references to god, spirit or higher power. This is quite intentional, and represents in fact a main thrust of my argument: *Alcoholics Anonymous* is replete with a wonderful and useful toolkit that can help anyone stay sane and sober if they are willing, even after we take out all the unnecessary, distracting, obfuscating religious language.) They may no longer be with us, but I suspect that Bill and Bob, Carl Jung, Dr. Silkworth and Chuck C. would all have been impressed by the correlation between this focus on a new pair of glasses and contemporary findings in the brain and behavioral sciences.

So, scientific findings support our experience: we can act our way into right thinking. We can ultimately enjoy lasting, whole scale changes in our personalities through seemingly small, incremental changes in behavior. Every time we experience a desire to drink and, instead, go to an AA meeting, call a friend, or work with a newcomer, we weaken that demon and strengthen that angel. We do the next right thing and, at some point, we realize that all these slow incremental steps have produced a significant, "miraculous" transformation. Our brain is literally being rewired, slowly but surely reprogrammed.

The AA tradition is to call this kind of change "spiritual" for two reasons. First, because of tradition. This sort of personal transformation, prior to the last couple hundred years of human history at least, was generally considered the sole province of religion, the handiwork of angels and deities.

Second, the caulk thing again. We find the radical change inexplicable, so we apply the magic, one-size-fits-all explaining power of theism as a metaphysical caulk in order to satisfy the never-ending human thirst for understanding or explanation.

Most importantly, these responses are not merely unnecessary; they are demeaning and disempowering in a very important sense. Our recovery is not up to angels, demons, or gods. It is up to us. We are responsible for taking the necessary actions that ensure the necessary changes which make for lasting, contented sobriety. Furthermore, supernatural explanations such as this give the false impression that we know all we need to about the phenomenon in question. As such, they tend to stand in direct conflict with the kind of curiosity and exploration which will grow the recovery sciences and our understanding of the relevant social and psychological processes.

The Real Higher Power

The most miraculous and inexplicable force at work in Alcoholics Anonymous may be fellowship itself. Even the most devoutly religious members depend upon our society, upon the power of the group. Often they will describe their fellow AAs, in a typical example of religious interpretation, as the mouthpiece through which god speaks to them. The fellowship is understood as a mere vehicle, or as a temporary expedient to be replaced by the real Higher Power when the newcomer finally "comes to" or "comes to believe". But the experience of most recovering alcoholics is that, what guides and sustains us on a day-by-day basis are peer support, empathy, mentor guidance, and the emotional reinforcement of group membership. In short, what keeps us sober from day to day is fellowship.

Consider these three suggestions, probably the most common ones made to an alcoholic who is suffering:

1. Go to a meeting

2. Call your sponsor

3. Work with another alcoholic

What do all three have in common? They all entail immersion in the society of recovering peers, a meaningful connection with our newfound tribe. Reams of data from social psychology, evolutionary biology and a host of other disciplines attest to the essential role played by peer groups and societies in determining both our values and our action choices, in shaping our thoughts and behaviors. Scientifically, mounting evidence suggests that the social group is the source of an important kind of basic emotional nurturance that is fulfilling to tribal hominids such as we at a most fundamental level.

Our brain evolved to be what it is over the course of five million years spent in small, familial tribes, within which complete immersion and total dependence were essential for our very survival. We are, at our core, not so much individual animals as we are pack members. Gathering in fellowship is the most important practical tool we have borrowed from religion and the church. But, in the end, the power of the group is undoubtedly a little less miraculous, a little more ancient, and a little more explicable, than once thought.

The tribe functions as the disseminator and teacher, the source of encouragement and reinforcement, that which empowers the addict to live a better life on a daily basis. The fellowship offers new ideas, role models who practice them, wise guidance and counsel, reinforcement of values and goals, and essential emotional rewards to its members. It empowers us to practice new and different behaviors until they become new and different habits. As time passes our membership within the tribe is the source of life enriching friendships.

But it also becomes an important source of a newfound sense of value and purpose as, over time, we transform into seasoned members who reap significant benefits from passing guidance and support on to the next member in need. This life sustaining mutual exchange is a huge part of recovery. It builds a web which sustains us all, a web of support that is fundamentally tribal. Our lives are saved, shaped and defined by the herd. We survive by running with the pack. The fellowship is the most tangible instantiation of a "higher power" in our lives. I would argue that we need seek no further.

For humans, isolation is death. Community is life. We overestimate the value of religious belief and faith in god: in fact, the community of fellows is the vehicle, whether it is church, temple, ashram, therapy group, mosque, sangha, a meeting of Alcoholics Anonymous, or the meeting after the meeting.

Keep in mind how miserable and close to disaster Bill Wilson was in spite of his life-changing experience at Towns Hospital. AA lore unwisely exaggerates his alleged spiritual experience. This was, in all probability, merely a side effect of the quasi-toxic, hallucinogenic Belladonna cure being administered at the time.

But when Bill went out into the world and engaged with other alcoholics, he ultimately found what he was looking for. It was not more white light, or god, or a higher power that he found, but a drunken country doctor named Bob. The lasting good they created is a society of peers who gain synergetic strength in numbers, loving support from each other, and much wisdom gleaned from years of collective experience.

A Wee Dash of Philosophy

For hundreds of years Euro-American thinking has been largely Hobbesian, by which I mean that we have a tendency to think of ourselves as individuals in a war of all against all. Of necessity, such excessively individualistic archetypes give rise to social contract theories. That is, we separate, warring individuals need something to come between us, to grease the social wheels, to ensure group cohesion. Otherwise a world of such flagrant self seekers would just degenerate into all out war. Morality is generally thought of as a variation on this social construct, by which we surrender selfish preferences in a compromise to retain a mutually beneficial social order.

But we are in a historically transitional period. Across a wide range of disciplines the Hobbesian view is being challenged. In the replacement paradigm we are no longer intrinsically selfish, with externally imposed, contractual forces serving to mitigate our otherwise unfettered covetous nature. We are, in fact, equally motivated by pro-social impulses from within. This school of thought is an offshoot of the insights of none other than Charles Darwin himself, amongst others, who observed that sympathy was a fundamental human emotion. Moral emotions, pro-social hunger, dependence upon the tribe, all of these things are hard-wired into us. We are as much inclined to cooperation as we are to competition. We may be innately aggressive, yet we are similarly predisposed to empathy, sympathy, and compassion. Individual powerlessness and dependence on the group are as definitive of who we are as is our much vaunted individuality.

If there is any truth to these thoughts, and an ever expanding body of scientific findings suggests that there is, we might come to some important conclusions. One is that immersion in fellowship offers us exactly the life-sustaining support we need, feeding us at a core level, bringing us an increased sense of personal value, purpose, emotional fulfillment and peace of mind. Rejoining the herd may be more scientifically life changing than old school thinkers would have thought.

The kindling, or rekindling, of essentially human pro-social emotions and behaviors is a large part of what we call recovery. Of course, recovery in this sense is a great deal more than putting the plug in the jug. It is about creating, or recreating, ourselves as comfortable members of a flock and, as such, comfortable human beings. In short, by gathering in herds and caring, in giving and cultivating an unselfish mentality, in becoming a part of, we are nurturing an essential aspect of ourselves as pack animals. We experience this in the fellowship of AA, and this extends out into "all our affairs", which means, of course, into the various families, tribes, packs and communities of which we are also members.

Religious tradition often depicts humanity as the source of all evil, while god is the source of all good. In any AA meeting around the country you can hear people mirror this view. We see "self will" as the source of all our troubles. But, when something really good motivates or befalls us, we are quick to give the credit to god. Whether religious or secular in its structure, this kind of thinking is just a variation on the aforementioned paradigm: humans are intrinsically selfish, weak or bad, while all good and healthy motivations come from outside of us, whether by some form of social contract or via the benevolent intercession of a supreme being.

I would like to suggest that we challenge this self-destructive viewpoint. Instead, let us recognize that a hunger for the good is an essential part of being human. God didn't invent AA or write the twelve steps. Desperate, hopeful humans did. God didn't bring us to AA. We came, beaten and bedraggled, because some unfulfilled part of us hungered for something better. God doesn't fix us. Immersion in fellowship, simple rules for right living, and our willingness to change are the things that fix us. And these things restore us to a sanity and balance that is completely, naturally human in every way.

The Butcher, the Baker, the Carpenter, and the Mechanic

When I walk into a meeting of the fellowship of Alcoholics Anonymous and participate with a teachable mind, I am working the first three steps to absolute perfection. There is no more to it than that.

In spite of the fact that I have been a clean and sober member for the vast majority of my adult life, I have been unable to, as they say, "come to believe" in anything more, such as an abstract, immaterial, or spiritual "higher power". Some very well intentioned old timers have worked extra hard to convince me that it was essential to my very survival that I come to believe in some form of capital G-God. In spite of years of effort on their part and mine, the only conclusion I have been able to come to is that I am an atheist. Nonetheless I am sober today, am a regular member of AA, and I work and live by a great many of the same principles that we all share. I just do not believe in God or anything like it in any form.

Moreover, I think it is unfair to refer to we atheists as "non-believers". I believe in many things. I believe in things for which there is solid evidence. For example, I believe in brain neuro-plasticity. The facts of neuro-science give me something reasonable to put my trust and hope in. It excites me to know that my old neural circuitry, and its concomitant destructive behavioral correlates, can atrophy and wither as my old behaviors fade into the past. It comforts me and gives me tangible hope to know that, each day that I do the right thing, attend meetings, remain clean, and live by codes of love and tolerance, my neural circuitry is being rewired to make such a sustainable lifestyle habitual and easier, and more and more natural to me.

I was told by those old timers that "We cannot think our way into right living, but we can live our way into right thinking". How pleased they would be, were they alive, to have this insightful slogan verified by modern science.

I also believe, as mentioned above, that our brains evolved to take the shape they currently have over the course of many millions of years in small family tribes on the African Savannah. In those millennia we were literally designed by nature to be tribe members. The individual is solitary, weak and insufficient. In other words: powerless. Immersion in a like-minded fellowship, while recently borrowed from the Oxford Group and other religious institutions, has much, much deeper roots. It is within our hard-wired nature to be members of a tribe. We are loved and, just as importantly, we love others. This is tremendously healing and empowering. The human connection is paramount.

I also believe that I am powerless over alcohol and drugs. Unlike many atheists I know, I do not have a problem with the concept of powerlessness. I believe most assuredly that I am powerless, and not just over alcohol and drugs, either. But I believe it is safe to say that, left to my own devices, I will drink and use again and, for this alcoholic, that means the difference between life and death. You see, I am a pretty low- bottom fellow, so there is no room for doubt. Sober, I have a chance to live long enough to have forty more years maybe, watch my kids grow up, get to know some grandkids maybe, enjoy a few thousand more sunsets and basketball games, plant some hibiscus, wait till they bloom, grow old with my beloved wife. On the other hand, if I pick up, I am disowned within days, dead within months. No margin for error.

With these beliefs, I have come to a very different understanding of atheism, powerlessness, and the first three steps. Step one is no problem. I am powerless, and my life is unmanageable by me. I work step two and three every time I walk into an AA meeting, interact with a fellow in recovery, or even when I read recovery-oriented literature, provided I am doing these things with humility, with an open and teachable mind.

You see, the fellowship of recovering persons is my higher power.

When I plug into the fellowship like this I am immersing myself in a like-minded tribe which shares the all important common goals and values of sustainable sobriety. As a consequence of plugging in, of connecting with the fellowship in this way, I am strengthened; I am given the power I need to live more successfully as a sober individual. In other words, alone I can become insane, but I make a habit of regularly hanging with you guys in a relatively teachable, humble state. I am more often than not restored to sanity when I do so. That's the first three steps in a nutshell.

The group is a valid higher power. Unlike Bill's implication in the chapter "We Agnostics", the fellowship is not merely a temporary substitute. It is, in fact, all the higher power we need. On any given day that my feet are made of clay, another individual may strengthen me with a smile, a handshake, a greeting or a hug. Another individual may serve to remind me of how bad it is out there still drinking. Another serves to remind me of how much harder it is to get clean than it is to stay clean. And yet another will articulately describe the process of recovery in a manner which reboots my own.

One member may be enjoying great benefits and expressing deep gratitude for the gifts of sobriety. Her gratitude and enthusiasm are infectious. We may all share a laugh at yet another fellow's tale, with its deeply familiar aspects. Another may describe the excellent benefits of continued sobriety in a manner which either reinforces my awareness, or maybe brings me renewed hope for future progress. And yet another might talk through their own sober struggle with a real-life problem in a way which strengthens me, or models for me, or reaffirms my own sober struggles, or just leaves me feeling grateful that I'm not her today. Or some guy's sharing may simply help him heal, as a problem shared with others does, and each of us tribe members benefit as active participants in this healing process.

These are just a few of the ways that my fellows lift me up daily and set my feet on the lifelong path with renewed conviction and energy. On any given day some of us will be weak in some, or maybe all, areas. But we can count on the larger tribe and its collective strength and wisdom to lift us up anew. I do not use the word spiritual to describe this, because, to me, the word spiritual is overused and meaningless. It is unclear and, like most religious language, unnecessarily vague and mystical. Imprecise at best. I do use the word synergy on rare occasion which, in spite of its new- agey tone, simply means that the whole is greater than the sum of its parts. Quite plainly, alone we are weak, together we are strengthened. The fellowship is my higher power, and it is the power of human tribal synergy.

When I plug into the fellowship through working the first three steps, I am applying scientific knowledge regarding the primacy of our tribal nature, as well as the cognitive sciences regarding neuro-plasticity and the ability of fellowship to, quite literally, change our minds. Our founding fathers were really onto something. More, in fact, than they could have realized.

So I am an atheist. But I do believe in the first three steps and in powerlessness. Bill tries, in "We Agnostics", to convince us to have an open mind because he hopes, as he believed it necessary, that we will all come around to believing in god more or less as he did. He thought, and his beliefs have held an inordinate sway over the subsequent generations, that belief in god was the only route to recovery. But even his idol Carl Jung understood the pivotal role of fellowship. In a letter Dr. Jung wrote to Bill Wilson in 1961, he wrote that unless surrounded by "the protective wall of human community ... an ordinary man ... isolated in society, cannot resist the power of evil..."

I suggest that we keep an open mind because, as we have learned from psychology, science, and the experience of men and women in recovery since the publication of the Big Book over 75 years ago, neither god, nor belief in god, are necessary for continuous recovery. Fellowship, community, support — "one alcoholic talking to another" — are the crucial elements to long-term recovery. God is not necessary for sustainable sobriety. It is optional only.

Ears and Sows

Honesty, Open-mindedness and Willingness to change are said to be the indispensable keys to recovery. H.O.W. has become most popular, as in "HOW it works". But this common expression of definitive values may be the result of nothing more than our curious obsession with acronyms. Sit in the rooms of AA long enough and somewhere along the line you are going to get your fill of acronyms.

But surrender is key, too. Why not the SHOW of recovery? This would most certainly apply to a number of our more character-filled meetings.

Why do we not praise S.O.W.? Unfortunately, most of us would agree that the SOW of Recovery just doesn't have the right ring to it.

Nonetheless, surrender is indispensable. This is the first of the six steps discussed earlier, the "complete deflation". We addicts experience key moments in which the limitations of self-will are recognized, consciously or not. An honest willingness to face our hindering self-faith arises. We enter a psychological state of newfound openness in which we become willing to let go of long-held beliefs, prejudices, and opinions. Generally a result of some form of personal calamity, hitting bottom with either the bottle or with some character defect running amuck in our lives, such moments of extreme duress and the subsequent recognition of limitation are sometimes followed by surrender, a newfound openness to change. Open-mindedness is intimately connected with surrender. They are both aspects of a transformative willingness, or willingness to transform, that is at the heart of recovery. These are all key aspects of hitting bottom, and subsequently embracing recovery, which are entirely explicable on secular grounds.

This hopeless condition and subsequent surrender is not the entire picture, however. Into this darkness a ray of light needs to shine. Most of us experience this in human form, generally another member of AA. Somewhere along the line we encountered some person or group of persons who had stopped the madness, maybe changed a bit for the better. These fellow humans are the seeds planted in our minds, waiting for the rains of despair to nurture them. Ebby T. was Bill's seed, Bill was Bob's, and so on down the line to you and me. This is how most of us come to AA. When we finally get here it is human sponsors and human-filled meetings and literature written by humans which guides us towards the light of recovery. The fellowship of AA is the life preserver which comes to our aid, prevents us from drowning in our sea of despair. God, religion and spirit just muddy the waters.

Did I mention that we also love metaphors?

Surrender is just one of the key elements in our toolkit. Many of these Essential Attributes of Recovery, we'll call them the E.A.R. just for fun, are traditionally associated with religion. But these EARs can be understood independent of religious belief. Consider, as a thought experiment, those "religious" persons you have known who fail to display the "spiritual" characteristics of humility or open-mindedness. Certainly each of us has encountered religiously devout members who are stubborn, too self-assured, or close-minded. Some embody the exact opposite of our essential qualities of HOW. Conversely, consider more secular persons you know who embody the EAR, independent of any religious belief. Certainly you know some very humble, honest, open-minded persons who, now that you think of it, have never uttered a word about god, spirit or higher power.

Another EAR we need to cultivate in order to successfully change our lives is humility. As may have occurred to you, this is also one I need to continue developing. But I know enough to say that humility is, on a simple level, merely awareness of the fact that, alone, we are weak. On our own most of us are unable to overcome a problem with the crippling magnitude of addiction. However, with the support of the society of recovery-oriented persons, our newfound tribe, we tap into a greater power which allows us both to get sober, and also to get on with the process of making the needed positive changes in our lives.

Humility entails the ability to truly know that we do not know, to be open to new ideas, practices, and beliefs. Bill Wilson himself, in the Big Book itself, says that "we know only a little" (p. 164), and suggests we have an open mind to new developments which will guide us in our recovery. Ironically, the more devout, religious members are often the ones who have the biggest problem with this sort of humility.

This is not coincidental. Religious thinking tends to stand in direct conflict with the kind of exploratory, curious thinking which, in my opinion, should be an important part of our lives as recovering persons. The more religious members I know tend to be overconfident in their beliefs, certain they are right about them, and sure that the rest of us must ultimately come around to their way of thinking if we wish to get things right.

Worse still, theists tend to believe their answers settle the important questions once and for all, bringing an end to the need for any further inquiry whatsoever. This is not humility.

Humility is genuinely believing that we know only a little. Humility is not a perspective which leads us into a mental cul-de-sac, but an open road stretching to the horizon. It leads not to overconfidence but to curiosity, wonder, and a thirst for exploration. We should be very interested in how we might better understand the recovery process, especially when we reflect on just how many of our brothers and sisters relapse or never get clean in the first place.

Surrender and humility are foundations for changing old patterns and replacing them with new ones. A willingness to do things differently arises. Inspired by the pain of desperation, these newly heightened psychological states, this SHOW, is where the true work is taking place. At first, this willingness expresses in simple things, like following directions: go to meetings, don't drink between meetings, get a sponsor, work the steps. Over time the meaning of surrender deepens and broadens to include a lasting and pervasive psychological attitude of acceptance. "We have ceased fighting anything or anyone" (p. 84) says the Big Book. More will be said below about this crucial state of mind when we discuss AA's "Let Go and Let God".

Honesty is also a big part of this process, and another EAR. As self deception is key to the ongoing behavior associated with active addiction, an essential component in the relevant psychic transformation is the reversal of dishonest patterns of thought, and their replacement with honest ones. The most essential first step in this newfound lifestyle: honesty about drugs and alcohol, their true role in the addict's life, and the impact of addiction on the people around them.

But other layers of self deception are peeled away as we continue to live by AA principles. We begin to see how alcohol and drugs are but a symptom of our disease, and start the lifelong project of getting real about our defects of character. We begin to practice honest self appraisal and confession with the fourth and fifth step, make lifelong practices of them in the tenth. This process of coming clean is psychologically and socially essential. In so doing, I start to become the kind of person I can live with, can feel better about being. My society begins to see me in a different light, and a new, healthier, more nurturing dynamic between self and society begins to develop. This dynamic cycle reinforces recovery. New habits start to put down deeper roots. The need to use chemicals begins to recede.

Service to others as a value, like confession, also receives plenty of association with religious traditions. Yet both can, and do, stand on their own two feet. From what has been said before, a fairly obvious argument for the value of service has to do with our definitively social nature. In direct antithesis to the self-involvement of active addiction, the recovery lifestyle involves, in the quintessential argument for "acting our way into right thinking", a high commitment to service towards our fellow humans. Caring about and actively helping others is a perfect antidote to the self obsession which characterizes the addict mind. In so doing we build the kind of nurturing, integrative social relations which support a sustainable recovery.

Additional therapeutic value is undoubtedly gained by the fact that, in service to other alcoholics, the addict's defects are magically transformed into assets. His pitiful past now serves as the springboard both for his new life and, of equal importance, for his newfound sense of value to the larger communities of which he or she is an integral part. This gives the recovering person a sense both of purpose and also of value. This is why so many recovering persons either "sponsor" or enter into recovery-oriented professional pursuits. Recovery is further reinforced by the fact that this purpose and value is grounded in his continued abstinence and participation in active recovery. Through service the addict engages in a cyclic reinforcement of benefits, good both for the recovering person and for the larger society of which he or she is a part. Everyone benefits from this new found mission to "carry the message" and "practice these principles in all his affairs".

These are just a sampling of the principles which guide our new lives. Upon closer inspection one can see that these EAR are not separate and distinct qualities, but interrelated, multifaceted and multi-layered. For example, when we first arrive honesty may mean being honest about drinking and drugs in our life, our powerlessness over them, their power over us. The next layer might be to start being honest with those around us about thoughts and urges and triggers. Another layer has us honestly facing the powerlessness and unmanageability in our lives as regards things other than the chemicals. Then we may find ourselves facing the real consequences of our behaviors on those around us with a newfound rigor.

The value of honesty continues to reshape our lives, our characters, and our behaviors, as, growing older in sobriety, we make a daily practice of self-reflection, owning our motives, confession of wrongful thoughts and choices, and continued honest observation and re-affirmation of individual powerlessness. The multi-layered and ongoing effects of embracing and fully living with these cultivated mind sets are definitive components of lifelong sobriety. Yet, to beat on the dead horse, none of them require that we believe in god, religion or spirit. They may require a "church" in a sense, as in a supportive fellowship of like-minded persons, but they do not require religion per se.

Am I being a hypocrite? After all, I am suggesting we need to be open-minded and surrender our old ideas. Yet I appear to be arrogantly critiquing 75 years of recovery methodology based upon old ideas I myself have clearly proven unable to surrender. May be a valid critique. But maybe not. It is also true that I have spent half of my life trying to be something I am not, trying to believe in something that, in my heart of hearts, has always felt to me like a lie and a fairy tale. I've worked for 25 years to surrender beliefs that are at the core of my being in order to follow AA's teachings. Throughout all these years I have fully engaged in the project, have been willing to let go of all my old ideas, have embraced religious pursuits, practices and ideas with desperation, passion and zeal. Only now has it occurred to me that I can surrender to those things that really make the difference, the psychological and social principles which are truly doing the work, without also surrendering reasonable and valid beliefs which, to me, are just plain old common sense, such as:

- Do not believe in anything for which there is absolutely no evidence.

- Do not believe in fairy tales, make-believe, or invisible best friends.

If we are to be truly open-minded, and most especially, if we are interested in furthering the cause of carrying the message to the many alcoholics and addicts who are still suffering, we should remain open to the possibility that god may be an outdated, antiquated human construct that, while essential to getting us this far on the path, can now be released, like training wheels from a youngster's bike, allowing us both to take greater responsibility for our own continued recovery, and to more successfully navigate the road ahead…

Oops. More metaphors. Sorry…

We Agnostics are not Broken

The word spiritual is used a lot in AA. We are taught that we need "to pick up the set of spiritual tools laid at our feet" (p. 25), that we must live by a simple set of "spiritual principles". But spirituality is a vague, even meaningless term. What exactly are we saying? Certainly the tools of recovery are very profound in their impact. They are all-encompassing. They change our actions, but more essentially our values, emotions, our entire lives even. They bridge the gap between the psychological and the social and are too big for either category. Being so all-encompassing and important, so big, it is understandable that the words to describe them might elude us.

I suspect that this is all there is to it. Spirituality, like god, is a concept we employ simply because we have come to the edge of our current understanding, have pushed no further, and it is at this point that our words fail us. Like our ancient ancestors facing a volcano or hurricane, our understanding of the processes at work is undeveloped, simple, riddled with caulk and imaginary filler. We are in awe and, quite literally, speechless, so we attribute the big thing before us to something magical or supernatural. Being in awe is fine, but it seems out of place when dealing with something so obviously medical, psychological, social, scientifically-understandable and, importantly, life-threatening as alcoholism and drug addiction.

Understanding that spirituality and god are terms employed when people have come to the edge of their comprehension helps me on a daily basis when I sit in AA meetings and listen. Whenever I hear god, spirit, or higher power, and can avoid falling into resentment or giving in to feelings of alienation, I try to think of it as a kind of shorthand for the life-sustaining, beneficent values, attitudes, and actions. I just delete the religious implications and substitute my own understanding. I have always had to do this. The difference for me this time around is that I no longer feel like I am cheating, or faking it, or hanging on until I finally "come to believe". This is it. I have arrived. I am exactly where I need to be. I am entirely at ease, even proud, to be an atheist.

Contrarily, the AA main line advises that, if we agnostics and atheists hang around long enough, we should eventually come around to the more religious point of view. We will "come to believe". Our higher power will now be called god. We may join or re-join an established religious tradition. Like it or not, this is a main theme in Alcoholics Anonymous. Quoting the tenth tradition does nothing to change this flagrant fact.

The chapter in the Big Book entitled "We Agnostics" is a very thinly veiled argument that some form of belief in god, however you can come to understand it, is necessary for recovery. In some ways the emphasis on open-mindedness in the Big Book points in exactly the opposite direction from mine. The Big Book seeks to gently guide the newcomer away from atheistic convictions and towards traditional religious beliefs. I am arguing that we keep an open mind because, contrary to core teachings, spirituality and god may be entirely irrelevant to recovery.

To go a tad farther, it may actually do addicts and alcoholics and our recovery a real disservice to rely on such nebulous concepts. They can mask our responsibility. The presumption that recovery is supernatural or divinely-inspired conceals our role in the project. Furthermore, we denigrate humanity and our natural capacity for positive change when we relegate our recovery to non-human, supernatural powers. Theistic

61

interpretations like that stand in diametric opposition to learning more about the psychology, social psychology and neuro-science of recovery. After all, if god is doing it, we need waste no time or energy trying to figure out how it works or how we can do it better. This strain of thinking, so prevalent in AA, explains the stony silence elicited by anyone who talks about recovery in terms of science, academic disciplines, or learning more and improving our understanding of the processes involved.

I've often heard talk about the magic of the higher power, him finding us parking spots, and door knobs as deities, all to murmurs of assent. But I have spoken about the excitement of the science of re-wiring our neural pathways and heard the proverbial pin drop.

The contemporary form of Judeo-Christian thought which predominates in AA suffers from a mistaken and highly pernicious assumption about human nature: people are inherently evil, and all good things come from god. This cultural habit, though fundamentally religious and distinctly Judeo-Christian, lives on in contemporary secular thought.

For many years the argument that humans are inherently selfish has held sway in both academic and popular discourse. We jumped enthusiastically upon misinterpretations of *The Selfish Gene* and the fact that chimpanzees were aggressive hunters and killers, confirmations that we are inherently bad beasts. Meanwhile, a few miles down the road, Bonobos were anonymously humping away, engaged in perpetual sexual social appeasements and a vast array of pro-social behaviors that equally illuminated our deeper nature, yet failed to make the evening news.

Only in our more recent history has a more scientifically-informed, balanced understanding developed. In this newer perspective we are of a more dual nature, inherently selfish, yet also innately altruistic, sympathetic, cooperative and compassionate. These pro-social qualities are not external, forced attributes, but inherent aspects of our human nature. Reminds me of a parable I heard at a Christian men's retreat once. The short form: A black dog and a white dog are at war inside of me. Which one is winning? Whichever one I feed.

In a nutshell, recovery is all about feeding the white dog.

In sum, we agnostics, atheists and non-believers are not only not broken, we may in fact be onto something. We may be the forerunners of a new way of looking at recovery which does not pass off responsibility to supernatural entities or processes, and which presupposes that radical transformation is an entirely natural, explicable phenomenon which can be cultivated and nurtured. From my point of view, the whole linguistic tradition of calling us "non-believers" is backwards. We do not play "make-believe" anymore, that is true. Yet we truly do believe: we believe in humanity, in human goodness, and in the innate human capacity for positive change.

A final philosophical, and decidedly conciliatory, point should be made here. We may all, in fact, be trying to do the same thing. All of us in recovery are trying to establish a closer connection with the real force, or forces, which bring about sustained recovery and a quality life. To some extent the argument is simply a semantic one. What name we ascribe to the life-sustaining principles does not so much matter. We are both seeking the power behind the throne. We may speak different languages, but we are all fellow travelers on the same path.

Let Go and Let God

Today I heard a great little story at my home group of Alcoholics Anonymous. The man sharing, whose name is not Joe but we'll call him Joe, was only 36 days sober. He recounted how he had gone to a family gathering to celebrate his grandmother's birthday. He'd parked his truck in a muddy ditch outside the house, and was immediately accosted by an "an angry, aggressive red neck".

The stranger was ready to get into a fight with Joe over his truck's proximity to a newly graveled driveway. Joe laughed, thinking the man was kidding. Of course this merely heated things up the more. As Joe headed up the family path, his sister emerged. The sister and the redneck neighbor, clearly with some less than pleasant history, proceeded to get deeper into it. At this point Joe, who has been striving to avoid a violent confrontation, begins to feel obliged to step in, as his sister is now being verbally abused.

Then suddenly a thought occurred to Joe. Maybe, he thought, I'll test this new AA stuff out and see if it really works. Instead of fighting, he calmly agreed to move the truck a few inches back, ameliorating the angry man. Simple enough. Problem solved, drama averted.

But the real AA lesson was in what happened afterwards. Joe let go. Period. He moved on. He went into the house, hugged his grandma, had something to eat, and let go of the whole episode.

His sister, on the other hand, remained flustered, apologizing repeatedly for the altercation. When it was time to depart, she again apologized. But Joe had let go. The incident no longer had any power over him, no longer aggravated him.

We alcoholics are disturbed by our capacity to re-sent, or re-feel. We cling to hurts, slights, fears, unfulfilled wants. We nurture them, fuel them, and build our characters upon them. Over time such destructive habits of thought can become deeply entrenched, our personalities sadly warped. One look at the world around us and you can see that this is not unique to alcoholics. It may, however, be more problematic for us than it is for most "normie's". It leads us to some very bad places.

In his story titled "Acceptance Was The Answer", Dr. Paul very effectively describes the essential role of a changed subjective state in ensuring the kind of emotional and mental stability we need to cultivate. This mental state of letting go, of acceptance, is a cure for much of what ails the alcoholic mind. His story contains some of the more popularly reiterated and practiced techniques for staying sober and not going crazy: Putting on a "new pair of glasses"; focusing on the good rather than the bad; emphasizing gratitude; talking about feelings; accepting persons, places, things and situations as they are; focusing our "courage to change" on "what needs to be changed in me and in my attitudes". (p. 417)

In a few simple pages some of the most profoundly useful tools of recovery are laid at our feet. For the purposes of my essay, two important conclusions can be derived. The first is that, while Dr. Paul does mention god, none of the oft cited tools he lays out rely upon religious/spiritual belief. Read it for yourself and you will see.

Secondly, Dr. Paul's story was not a part of the founder's ideas, not even a story that made it into the first edition of the Big Book. Yet his ideas are very popular in AA and help many people to contented sobriety. This means that AA is growing and changing, and that is both an important point, and a good thing.

The program for recovery from alcoholism and addiction was not so much set in stone in the 30s as it was set in motion. This is a big part of what I am arguing, in that AA has successfully added many new tools to its tool kit, all of which are now all available to us, and many of them do not require faith, magic, or ambiguities like spirituality.

Dr. Paul makes a forceful case for why and how we alcoholics and addicts might release our death grip on the universe. We cannot long live sober and contented lives without changing this pivotal mindset. We, who have struggled with our world for so long, trying to shape it to fit our tastes, twisting our emotions and our relationships into malignant knots in these vain and pointless pursuits, have finally begun to awaken to our proper place in the scheme of things. Acceptance and letting go are humility in action, or inaction as the case may be. Serenity, the very peace of mind that allows us to live long, contented, sober lives, stems directly from developing this humility, this ability to healthily, constructively detach from the things that disturb us.

Clearly we needed to cultivate this new way of thinking. But, for this alcoholic, "Let go and Let God" always felt like make-believe, like a game of pretend. The good news for the atheistically inclined is that we do not need to Let Go and Let God. We simply need to Let Go. Period. No god required. We do not need to turn over the universe to a deity. We simply need to turn it over.

Interestingly, it may be the case that turning over control of the universe to a self-conceived deity is actually a way of seeking to retain some measure of control. Let Go and Let

God still has a rider on it. After all, it is our own conception of god to whom we are letting go. So when we turn it over to god "as we understand him", we are really still hanging on. We are saying, in effect, I will surrender control of the universe to something I believe will do right, will do what is best, will manage things well, or some variation on a similarly consoling scenario.

This may be a soothing expedient, a way of introducing the principle of letting go to someone who is not habituated to doing so. After all, it is easier to let go when we believe that some benevolent force is going to take over the reins and make sure things come out as they should. But is this truly a deep faith? Or does it still retain a self referential quality, a kernel of control? Maybe not self will run riot, but self will thinly veiled?

The conditional surrender that is "Let Go and Let God" runs the risk of leading to some very disheartening experiences. When bad things happen to good people who believe in a just, all-powerful god, they are often taken aback. I have a personal story to tell along those lines as well, but will spare you this time.

The deity of our understanding is supposed to be looking over everything. It is supposed to be making sure, as a benevolent puppeteer would do, that all comes out well. Bad things are supposed to happen to bad people, good to good. Most believers believe in some kind of "karma". But this isn't how the real world works, and believing it is just sets us up for a fall.

The more religious members of AA hold that "nothing in god's universe happens by mistake". God cares for us, and the universe is designed to aid us in our spiritual growth and development. Everything is ordered, everything has a purpose. These beliefs are very important to the theistically inclined, and serve an important purpose of emotional consolation. But sometimes they may serve no other role than to comfort. If so, then, as Bill W. himself is oft quoted, we must be wary when, at times, we allow the good to be the enemy of the best (12 & 12, p. 138). Ironic though it may sound, belief in god may sometimes actually stand in the way of true surrender, deep acceptance, and the all important learning to let go to what actually is.

One of the goals of recovery should be to mature sufficiently that we can be OK without the surrogate controller role that god often plays. As an atheist I surrender to whatever is. If it turns out that there is no creator, I'm fine. If it turns out that "life originated out of nothing, means nothing, and proceeds nowhere" (p. 49), which Bill articulates as if it were a self-evidently hideous eventuality, I am OK with that.

Scientific findings do not threaten my understanding of things. In fact, they add to the glory, majesty, and wonder of things. They add elements of positivity and hope for the future, as opposed to a desperate clinging to tradition and the ways of the past. And if, when I die, I am no more than worm food and, hopefully, some very fond, lingering memories in the minds of those I've touched, so be it. It would be nice if there were a heaven and I got to live on forever and ever, preferably with forty virgins and a nice set of wings. But my surrender cannot be mitigated by consoling beliefs, cannot be contingent upon comforting imaginings. I need to turn it over to whatever is, as is, whether it fits my imaginary schema or not.

In conclusion, I must once again proffer the argument that our conservative, religious perspective as AA members might be standing in the way of our effectiveness. Theorizing or speculating are, as a general rule, mistrusted and frowned upon in Alcoholics Anonymous. But some of us are curious about the whys, and that may be a good thing.

For example, why are alcoholics prone to death-by-resentment? Do we actually learn to nurture resentments and subsequently cultivate the dubious skill of working ourselves into a tizzy in order to rationalize our drinking? By practicing this self-destructive mental habit we could feel more or less perpetually wronged. As the world will rarely, if ever, comply with our exacting standards, we can look forward to a constant string of disappointments, each offering up a satisfying justification for a good bout of self pity, rage, and a well-justified, all-out bender.

Or, conversely, are we wired this way, prone by nature to resentment? I have not studied the issue, but I would guess that alcoholism is physiologically and psychologically related to Obsessive-Compulsive Disorder. Speaking for myself, anecdotally, they seem to share a lot of similar characteristics. If so, then this would help to explain why resentment is so problematic for us, and learning acceptance so very important. Learning to let go is especially challenging, and especially freeing, for people with such forms of mental disease.

Secular recovery paradigms encourage research and investigation into these types of questions. Increased knowledge and understanding might help us develop a deeper, richer toolkit. We might be able to help more alcoholics and addicts into lasting recovery. But chalking such things up to the work of an unfathomable higher power does nothing to increase our understanding. Eschewing superstition may be important to our more effectively carrying the message to the still suffering alcoholics and addicts out there.

Set in Motion, Not Set in Stone

Alcoholics Anonymous is a temporary phenomenon. It is a historically contextualized response to a problem, or constellation of problems, which existed way before 1939, and will probably be with us well into the foreseeable future. Again, not an academic paper here, and I am not super well-informed on the history of treatment modalities through the ages.

But I know enough to see that AA is constrained, both in terms of temporal resilience and cross-cultural accessibility, by its heavy Judeo-Christian emphasis. Taking atheism seriously, and in particular the "Recovery Sciences", is not really a threat to AA. On the contrary, such an approach is all about taking what works in AA and expanding upon it, a synthesizing approach which guarantees the kind of elasticity and flexibility which will ensure the survival of the best of what AA has to offer for the generations to come.

We knew very little about alcoholism in 1939. While there is a sense in which we do not know *much* more today, we do know more, and a great deal more knowledge will be acquired and applied in the future. AA should be flexible, vibrant, and vital in order to stand the test of time, to work even better in the days, years, and decades to come. Rather than stagnate on 80 year-old ideas, some of which may be well beyond their prime and may significantly limit our effectiveness, we should strive to synthesize and grow. Let us be quick to see where the non-religious people are right, and make use of what *they* have to offer.

As individuals in recovery, we are taught that stagnation equals death. Members are told to remain active in the program, "green and growing" as some say, or face sober misery and the potential for relapse. One often hears that the recovering alcoholic is either moving away from a drink or towards one. We are used to this idea, of stagnation as death. Maybe this is true for AA as an institution as well.

All of this may be true, yet we owe a great debt of gratitude to religion. This is where I find most atheists to be entirely off- track. Most atheists I have encountered are more virulently anti-theist than a-theist. While I believe in the kind of conciliatory view that rationally, objectively acknowledges the strengths of both sides, I fear my writings are ultimately doomed to the scrapheap for lack of accessibility. I am too critical of god, religion and spirituality to be understood by most AA members, who will undoubtedly feel threatened by what I say in these pages. Yet I am also too appreciative of religion to be accepted by most atheistically-inclined readers, many of whom angrily abhor AA as a cult of the worst kind and are prone to freak out when they hear the word "prayer".

But I say we thank god. Thank god for AA. Religion was prominent before AA. This is where most of our founding members got their ideas. I, for one, am grateful for what has been handed down to us, the guidance and direction proffered by religion in getting us this far along the path. The importance of fellowship, for example. This obviously pre-dates religion. Understanding the deep and essential role of community, peer, and tribe in recovery is vastly important. Evolutionary biology and social psychology will continue to offer us insights in that direction. But its current practical role in recovery stems directly from religious traditions like Christianity, the Oxford Group in particular. Confessional: straight from Catholicism. Prayer: speaks for itself, and remains a valuable tool even for atheists like myself.

Meditation: much to be gleaned from Buddhism, the basics are often taught at treatment facilities. Yoga: deeply intertwined (get it?) with religious tradition, this is now commonly introduced at treatment centers as well. Both of these quintessentially religious practices are fairly common, albeit in rudimentary form, both in treatment facilities and amongst many contemporary recovering folk as aspects of their recovery program. Their inclusion speaks to the importance of religious traditions in offering us valuable tools. Yet they also speak to the fact that we can incorporate new ideas. And, both Yoga and meditation are practices that stand on their own, without any need for the often-associated complex theistic belief systems.

Many of the values so essential to our new way of life have traditionally been associated with religious teachings, and, for that, we owe a debt of gratitude as well. Surrender, humility, service to others, these are quintessentially religious values. Another example is the seven deadly sins. One is not generally thankful for sins, at least not when thinking of them as sins, that is. But it turns out this classic list is a fairly comprehensive enumeration of our most glaring shortcomings. As such, they offer us a handy guide for taking our inventory, and for getting a handle on our less than desirable repetitive character traits, and so, what we need to change in our thinking and our behavior. These are all key components in the process of moving away from our destructive propensities and towards what some people call a more spiritual life. I prefer to say that such things are keys to a more rewarding, fulfilling, and meaningful life, as I find the concept of "spirituality" suffers from both terminal ambiguity and terminal overuse, perhaps relatedly.

So, if I am so filled with gratitude, why rant at all? Because I genuinely believe that religious belief is an antiquated, outdated, and ineffective vehicle for conveying these important values and practices. Religion was once needed to understand the stars, before astronomy. It was once needed to explain volcanoes, until geology. Plate tectonics was not even "discovered" until the last century. Demons and angels were needed to explain our behavior. Exorcisms and burnings no doubt were performed on our very kind.

Maybe it is time to separate the wheat from the chaff. Keep the fundamental principles embodied in the steps, keep the fellowship, the peer "influence", the HOW's, the EAR's, the SHOW's. But lose the faith healing and the tendency to create an environment hostile towards empirical observation and study. God's services are no longer required.

Like a ferry boat that has taken us safely across the river, when its work is done, we eventually disembark and walk freely on the other side. We do not curse it when its work is done, nor do we return to it. We are thankful it has taken us on that one part of the journey. And now it is time to move on. And we simply go.

Likewise, we can be thankful for that one memorably excellent teacher we had in high school. But we don't go back and sign up for her class again and again and again.

Am I missing something? Is there something irreplaceable, some aspect of religious belief that cannot be co-opted by secular means with either equal or greater efficacy? I rack my brain, and I come up with only one thing. The great fact that atheists must confront is that, for us humans, comfort trumps truth. Religious belief is comforting, and the comfort it offers is often more important to people than cold, hard reality.

The strongest critique of my argument is that religious belief offers considerable emotional and psychological consolation and reassurance to those that believe. Somehow, turning things over to god is more comforting than turning things over to fate, nature, time, or other such impersonal, uncaring forces of the universe. While I believe that this was touched upon in the above section on god concepts having a self-referential quality, I also freely admit this is nonetheless a problem for my ravings. The comfort afforded by faith in traditional gods may be very important to help us sensitive sickos get through the day in one piece.

There is that, and there is also the very mighty and powerful placebo effect. Sometimes just believing can really, really help. We walk into an AA room, and we join in, doing what others do and parroting what others say. The great power of placebo ensures that we will think ourselves healed. And if we think ourselves healed, well, perhaps that's all that really matters, in 'it?

But we must consider the price of holding onto such beliefs. How important is the comfort we get from theistic interpretations if they stand in the way of our maximal effectiveness, our accessibility, our ability to reach those in need? Are being intransigent and emotionally soothed more important than creating a genuinely all-inclusive environment, one which encourages inquiry, investigation, and synthesis?

From the religious point of view, the problem of alcoholism is completely solved. They turn a blind eye to our abysmal 5% success rate, to the non-believers who don't make it. From their point of view, any further inquiry on recovery methodology is, by and large, considered to be pointless. You may think this an exaggeration, but think again.

How open is your group to any "sharing" which places an emphasis upon new modes of recovery, new ideas outside those in the Big Book or AA tradition, scientific findings, or atheist re-interpreting? At best, such "sharings" are genially tolerated. But the pressure to conform is very strong indeed. We should strive to create an environment which is more inclusive and diverse, more encouraging of the social and psychological curiosity and inquiry which are appropriate to our global culture and modern times.

If it ain't broke, don't fix it, we like to say. What if this is less a wise aphorism than an expression of our fear of change? Let us not forget that the vast majority of alcoholics and addicts do not live clean and sober, but suffer and die at the hands of our disease. I fully understand the fear and the resistance to change. Facing death as a black and empty abyss of nothingness sucks emotionally. I'd rather go to heaven too. Sometimes I feel lonely and afraid, and I wish I could believe as the devout do. But for atheists like me, the truth trumps the comforting beliefs.

In the end, perhaps ironically, I genuinely believe that we should have more faith. We should have faith that this thing can withstand some change, can grow and develop with our understanding. In this sense, atheism requires a greater faith than belief in god. Faith that we are OK, will be OK, as we are, without big daddy in the sky looking over us. We need to have faith that this thing we have can withstand change and still work. Atheism takes a very strong kind of faith, a faith that allows us to face life exactly as it is, not as we imagine or hope it to be.

Faith and belief are not the sole possession of the theistically inclined. Upon my return to recovery in AA, coupled with my newfound acceptance of myself as an atheist, I found no consolation whatsoever in religious or spiritual claims. In fact, they just served to confuse or irritate me. I did, however, find considerable emotional consolation in some decidedly cold, hard facts. For example, readings in neuro-science, to which I referred in earlier pages, greatly consoled me when urges to use drugs or alcohol would wash over me. "This too shall pass" and "Fake it till you make it" helped me.

But with the force of some real hard science behind them, these mere colloquial expressions acquired the force of some very real, absolutely reliable facts about being human and learning new habits. These described physiological processes were taking place within me each day I chose to live sober, each day building upon the past in a manner which promised improvement and eventual relief from the need to use. As an atheist, I find such genuine scientific findings not just interesting or informative, but also consoling, encouraging, and uplifting, while "god could and would if he were sought" just sounds like a childish, hollow lie.

If this is true, then I have faith, too. For example, I believe in the fellowship, in the power and wisdom of the group, in the radical transformation that takes place within us when we practice these principles in all our affairs. This new lifestyle promises, if I keep close to it, to carry me towards better days, towards wellness, away from dis-ease. I believe in this process, and with good reason. This is not a blind faith. I believe in it because I see it work in you and in others, and ultimately I see its effect in my own life. But this belief gives me hope and the promise of better things to come which helps to sustain me emotionally on a daily basis.

All of this serves to prove my point, which is, if belief and faith are essential subjective states regardless of whether it's god or a doorknob or the ocean or the fellowship or the EAR that we have faith in, the bottom line is that god, religion and spirituality are not necessary. We need to have that belief in a higher power, but, once again, our HP need never be god, religion or spirit. It is the state of mind within us, whether we call it belief or faith, which is the key determinative factor. In other words, god does nothing, yet belief and faith themselves are all-important. It is they that are doing the real work of recovery, the real heavy lifting.

We should beware not to cling blindly to what has worked in the past. If it points us in a new direction, we must have the courage to walk that path. We should be wary that religion and tradition might blind us to the potential for positive growth and change. We can stride forward with hearts full of faith and certainty that, armed with the excellent tools of sobriety, we can incorporate into recovery methodology the many new insights and discoveries of psychology, social psychology, psychiatry, therapy, and the brain and behavioral sciences. Just as Bill chose to synthesize the best of the Oxford principles with the insights of the medicine and psychology of his day, we can similarly incorporate the best of the past with our growing understanding of the recovery process. Doing so might enable us to carry the message of recovery with greater effectiveness.

These are the kind of thoughts that concern me at times. But there are times when I take a much more conciliatory view. At those times I am confident that we can walk side by side, theist and atheist alike, comfortable to live and let live. Different tools work for different people at different times in their lives. I am entirely *for* an all-inclusive approach to recovery. I have known the multiple hells of addiction, and would wish them on no one. Anything that works to get us free is fine by me.

It is not my intent to needlessly disparage religion's role in recovery. Mostly, I simply wish to pave the way for myself and others to fully embrace recovery without the hesitation or doubt associated with being agnostic or atheist. I want to be able to come out of the closet as a non-believer in AA, and I want other members, especially newcomers, to know that belief in god, religion, or spirit are not as fundamental to sustained recovery as many AA members suggest they are. Contrary to AA doctrine, being atheist or agnostic is not a malady which we must eventually overcome in order to achieve lasting, contented sobriety.

When all is said and done, I need to let go of all these strongly held opinions and ideas, and get on with the business of sober living. I need to go to meetings, where I will hear talk of god and spirituality. I need to be OK with the fact that no one will ever read these musings. I will never share about them at group level. They will be my little secret. I will pray, because it calms and comforts me, and sometimes I need that. I will go to meetings and strive with all the effort I can muster to keep an open mind to whatever is said. Interestingly, since coming to accept the fact that I am an atheist, I have felt LESS frustrated and alienated by the religious language used in AA meetings. Every time someone uses religious language, without fail, I find myself able to calmly interpret what they say and understand their sharing in my own secular manner. I am no longer doing battle, with them or within myself. I have finally achieved a measure of peace as regards this integral subject. Now I can get on with life. This project is over now.

Or is there another layer of the onion to peel…

Broaden the Circle Without Breaking the Bond

- Marya Hornbacher

The bulk of *Common Sense Recovery* was written when I was fresh out of The Camp, a small, local rehab where I once spent 28 days getting off the alcohol, weed, norco, vicodin, oxy, whatever I could lick off the floor, you name it. They did a nice job of drying me out and re-introducing me to the fellowship of Alcoholics Anonymous, within which I had previously enjoyed 23 years of continuous, uninterrupted sobriety. I wrote the manuscript entirely for myself, to get clear on how I had, and would hopefully once again, survive as an atheist within a Christian fellowship which, for some strange reason, denies that it is a Christian fellowship. The writing helped me.

But then something amazing happened to me. I discovered that I was not alone. I will never, ever be one of those old curmudgeons who bemoan modern technology and change, as I truly believe that the internet may have literally saved my life. It put me in touch with thousands and thousands of other atheists, agnostics and free-thinkers in recovery. This has begun a radical change in my life. I still attend about three local meetings a week here at home. While there, I still feel like a spy, and I still have to do a lot of atheist re-interpretation of what I hear.

But I am different now in quite a few ways, and this chapter is all about those changes.

The final chapters of this little book are mostly about what people like you and me can do. Some of us are more activist and outspoken than others. So pick and choose the ones that resonate with you. Come up with some new ones on your own. I'm sure my ideas are but the tip of the iceberg.

Strive to never let yourself become discouraged. Remember that butterfly flapping its wings somewhere far away? You absolutely never know what effect you are having on others. The smallest little actions can often have an endless rippling effect which literally goes on forever. Yes, you too can make huge, sweeping changes, simply by saying a genuine, welcoming hello to a newcomer.

To steal from our much beloved Big Book, consider that, in the poorly entitled "How it Works", Bill reminds us not to get discouraged. "No one among us has been able to maintain anything like perfect adherence to these principles." All we are after is a little right effort and a lot of forgiveness. Progress rather than perfection.

Dr. Bob also thought along these lines. Just after emphasizing the central role of genuine one-on-one human interaction in recovery, he begins to wrap up his story with this: "If you really and truly want to quit drinking for good and for all, and sincerely feel that you must have some help, we know that we have an answer for you. It never fails, *if you go about it with one half the zeal you have been in the habit of showing when you were getting another drink.*"

So, first of all, I have stopped silently sitting in rooms and insecurely interpreting my way to sobriety, thinking and feeling like I was weird and alone in the world. I know you are out there. You know that I am here. Now we know for sure that we are not alone. That is a super-empowering fact.

There is even a movement underway. This is a movement I am proud to be a part of. Even though I freely admit that I am not the activist sort, I will gladly confess that I do some of the things mentioned below. If a frightened, needy, overgrown child like me can do them, well, then, you most certainly can.

The first difference is that I have internalized a sense of a kind of injustice, a little resentment, if you will, towards Alcoholics Anonymous for being two-faced. For saying it's open to all kinds, but in reality being about divine intervention and the development of faith in the supernatural.

I have this newfound, strong conviction that people like me should not have to struggle as did I. In fact, most would not. They would simply give up. And I am afraid that is what most do. For some, that might not be a big deal. For alcoholics and addicts like me, though, that's a death sentence.

Action number one may be get on the web. Start interacting with other atheists, both in recovery and not. Spend time on sites like AA Beyond Belief (aabeyondbelief.org) or AA Agnostica (aaagnostica.org) and really read the things you find there. Interact with those you find there. This is something I do now, and it is an important new part of my recovery. Not only are you not alone anymore, but you are going to learn and grow like never before, and your recovery and knowledge will be greatly enhanced.

Next, after discovering all of us online, I went to my first ever convention. I know: a quarter of a century in AA with no conventions. Suffice to say I am not much of a people person. There are two tests I have scored perfect on in my life: 12 questions to find out if you are an introvert, and AA's twenty questions.

Anyway, while there, one activity my dear wife, Laura Joy, and I engaged in was to poll attendees as to what they thought was the most important action they could take to bring about much needed change in AA. What do you think the winning answer was?

I am going to tell you in just one second. But first I'm going to tell you an answer that did not win, perhaps distressingly. I was somewhat shocked, and a bit saddened, because, upon reflection, I think it is the single most important, not to mention obvious, answer of them all. That answer? Talk to the newcomer.

This is gigantic. Be the one who walks up to them after the meeting and checks in with them, asks them how they are doing, no matter how crossed their eyes are or how much they smell. I am going to. Listen to them rant. That's what most of them want. To be heard, listened to, to have someone care. If they have a problem with the "god stuff", all the better. "We will not regret the past nor wish to shut the door on it… we will see how our experience can benefit others. That feeling of uselessness and self pity will disappear. We will lose interest in selfish things and gain interest in our fellows…" Be prepared to let them know clearly, and in no uncertain terms, that their theistic status is entirely irrelevant to their membership and to their recovery from alcoholism. Get to them before the god people do, so that they can know the full range of options.

So, what was the winning answer? Start a new agnostic/atheist AA meeting. There is a great deal of information available on how to do so, and I can add little to that. Look on the internet. AA Agnostica even has a button you can press which will help you get this process underway. You will begin the all-important process of connecting with other likeminded folk in your area. Another excellent resource to read on such efforts is *A History of Agnostic Groups in AA* by Roger C. (available on the AA Agnostica website).

Go to these meetings. There are almost 200 agnostic AA meetings now, mostly all started in the last two decades. Go visit them. Take along some like-minded folk, enjoy the drive and the meeting, then have an informative chat with the founders afterwards. Find out how others have done it. Support them, and learn from them. Then you'll be ready to get started.

This is a great place to point out that politics can make strange bedfellows. Unite with others of the many different kinds who advocate for a similarly all-inclusive application of the third tradition. I was startled, as a scientific, materialist atheist, when I got to know some of the "spiritual" and "mystical" perspectives I encountered at the first-ever We Agnostics, Atheists, and Free Thinkers (WAAFT) International AA Convention. I did not know that one could be a Buddhist Atheist, as most practicing Buddhists indeed have their share of deities, prayers, and superstitions. But lo and behold, I met a self-described Buddhist Atheist in Santa Monica. And we found some very important common ground, indeed.

Moving forward, it is very important that we make clear we are not trying to create a new fellowship or cause a schism within AA. There still exists a very legitimate need for men's groups and women's groups, for gay groups and a variety of other specialty groups within our singular fellowship. It may be the case that, at some point, religion will truly be, as the tenth tradition suggests, an "outside issue". At that point, as John L. suggested, "AA members who wish can practice religion PRIVATELY". There may be Buddhist meetings and Catholic meetings for those so inclined.

But in these early stages of our movement we may well be the ones who have to give a little. It may well be that the next best step will be the creation of more and more similarly "themed" Alcoholics Anonymous groups for we agnostics, atheists and free thinkers. In such contexts we will be free to talk about our recovery in entirely secular terms, free to vent a little about our strong doubts and disbeliefs, and perhaps even get just a little chip off our shoulders about religious AA once in a while.

But let that last line not be left standing unaddressed. It would be highly divisive as well as individually pointless should meetings become just opportunities for religion bashing. "Getting it off your chest" happens. But counter-productive wallowing in resentments is not the same thing as recovery.

Plus, we must always remember our essential unity and our third tradition. Remember that the newcomer must always come first. Perhaps the most important point is that they should be made to feel safe, to feel like they have entered into an arena in which they are free to explore their own spirituality or lack thereof. "Religion bashing" can be just as ugly as "atheist bashing".

I have changed my religious status a dozen times at least since joining AA. I feel like I have finally settled. I am more comfortable and less restless than ever now that I am an atheist. It feels wonderful. But that's just me. We must allow each newcomer the freedom and the space to move through the various phases according to their own needs and at their own pace. And, dare I say it, not just the newcomers either. Who knows? You may be an agnostic today, an atheist, a Muslim or a Wiccan tomorrow.

So start an agnostic group in your town, or join one and support it. But remember to never let it get ugly. Let us not create an environment in which people are expected to conform to our agnostic, atheistic or free thinking ideals. Beware lest we find that we have seen the enemy, and he (or she) is us.

We must be examples of what we want to see: mutual respect, maturity, humility, acceptance of diversity, love and tolerance at all times. Build in a reminder or a by-law, read at the beginning of each meeting, which reminds us that we are not about religion-bashing. That will get us nowhere, even if the venting sometimes feels good for a brief moment.

> *Our membership ought to include all who suffer from alcoholism. Hence we may refuse none who wish to recover. Nor ought AA membership ever depend upon money or conformity. Any two or three alcoholics gathered together for sobriety may call themselves an AA group, provided that, as a group, they have no other affiliation.*

I spoke with my regional correspondent for our GSO the other day in order to try and get a clearer sense of exactly how things work. My main concern had to do with our new, agnostic AA meetings being easy to find and accessible, both for newcomers and everyone else as well. In other words, it had to do with being "listed".

Now, some discussion was had at the WAAFT Convention that, with the development of new technologies and the growing familiarity of people with alternative forms of communications technologies, the AA Central Office's "lists" may prove less and less authoritative and relevant over time. This may be true. Many of us are finding each other in new and different ways now. Nonetheless, for the moment, being officially listed still counts for something.

So here is what you may want to know regarding being officially "listed" as an Alcoholics Anonymous meeting. The bad news: if you hang "adulterated", "adjusted" or "alternate" steps on your walls, you run a high risk of being de-listed. The good news: each group is allowed to follow its own conscience as far as what it utilizes to engender discourse or what literature it chooses to place on its literature table. So, yes, if you're with me, this means the odd fact that you can read alternate steps and discuss them, but you cannot hang them on the wall. So be it, I can work with that.

I am working with another fellow I met at the conference and we are planning to start a meeting nearby, as there are none as of yet in our immediate area. Currently, we are going to follow his suggestion of having it be a speaker discussion format, with nothing debatable on the walls. We will work together to find readings for our literature table. We will find something to add whatever ritualized components we feel are needed to start and end the meeting.

Another idea would be to have a literature format meeting. For example, in one of my current favorite meetings we read a portion from "As Bill Sees It". This, as you can imagine, can get pretty dated and pretty debatable. You may wish to consider using the following:

1. *Beyond Belief: Agnostic Musings for 12 Step Life*. Joe C. has put this together and it serves as an excellent day at a time type book along the lines of *24 Hours a Day, Day by Day,* or *As Bill Sees It*. Great for discourse starters in a free-thinking meeting format.

2. *The Little Book: A Collection of Alternative 12 Steps*. This collection by Roger C. would be a great tool for getting discussion started in a meeting.

3. *The Alternative 12 Steps: A Secular Guide To Recovery*. This one, by Martha Cleveland and Arlys G., is just a great book to read, but could also serve as an aid in generating meeting topics.

4. Lest we not forget, there is already one which minimizes the god parts and is very practical right within our "conference-approved" hands: *Living Sober*.

So, one thing that is obvious at this point is that I have a limited range of experience. Remember, by my own admission, I just recently came out of a cave. Amongst the first things I found was AA Agnostica, and my world exploded very nicely. But there is much more out there, I am sure. I acknowledge this limitation in my exposure.

So, do what I do. Use the internet, search out new places, try, err and try some more. Some of it will be garbage, some of it will be jewels. Above I have listed some of the tools I have found in my search. Let's keep sharing and adding to the list. What are some resources you have found beneficial as you have tried to search for support as an atheist, agnostic or free thinker in recovery?

Walking the Talk

So, let's get back to that little poll that Laura Joy and I were taking. What was the second most popular answer? The second most popular answer was the one that I put first on my own list of actions to take. I believe it is one tiny action which is huge in its ramifications. That is, come out. Become open to your meeting about being an agnostic, a god-doubter, or an atheist.

I prefer atheist for a couple of reason. The chances that there exists anything remotely like their puppeteer god are extremely unlikely, and I am willing to bet on the side of certainty that it does not exist. I know what I believe. Second, it sends a strong, confident message. I am not "still thinking about it" or "trying to figure it all out" or "unsure of what I believe". There are excellent arguments for going with the whole range of titles, I believe. So, for me this is simply a matter of personal choice.

Atheist, agnostic or free thinker, coming out is a lot bigger than it sounds. First of all, many people are like me: the social acceptance and tribal embrace are a very key part of what helps us in recovery. So "coming out" may be in direct conflict with our most valued source of strength: our fellowship. You run that scary risk of saying "I don't believe in your God", and then being cold shouldered by your support system.

People will have different stories. All I can say is that I found it not nearly so catastrophic. I felt so conflicted, so scared the first time I stood up and said it in front of the whole group. I was surrounded by my "support group", my tribe, 60 or 70 guys who I generally wanted to love me, or at least like me. But, on the other hand, I was deeply committed to the truth.

88

To thine own self be true, right? So I stood up in front of the Roxas mens Group of Alcoholics Anonymous and I said "My name is Adam, and I'm an alcoholic. I am also an atheist."

The sky did not fall. No one heaved rotten tomatoes at me or shouted "heathen" or bared a large wooden cross. In fact I think I heard a few people mutter something like "duh" or "so what else is new". But I know that every one of us who comes out like this makes it a little more "normal", that is, familiar, not strange or exotic, just another part of daily life. And this process of normalizing atheism, just as with the historically recent efforts at "normalizing" LGBTQ, is a big part of making atheism no big deal.

And making it no big deal is a really big deal as we move in the right direction. Right?

So I think one of the most important things you can do is to simply come out, come out, wherever you are.

Say "I am an atheist and not missing out on anything".

Say "I am an agnostic and I am OK with that".

Say, "I do not believe in god, and I am comfortable that this is NOT a shortcoming in my program of recovery".

"I came; I came to; and I came NOT to believe."

Of course, every group and every region and every individual is unique. There is no way of guaranteeing what kind of response you will get. Be careful and be wise. But even if you get hostile or negative responses, remember that you may be the only example of an atheist AA this person will ever meet. Show them that, without god or religious faith, we can still be loving and tolerant and practice these principles in all our affairs. Counter hostility with patience, tolerance, forgiveness and love.

I remember reading once how a black woman was teaching her black son how he had to do just a little bit better, behave just a little less threatening, be just a little more polite than all his white peers. He became angry and vehemently responded "That is totally unfair." To this his mother responded, saying "Yes, son. It is definitely terribly unfair. But it is true nonetheless. If you wish to get the same grade, avoid the pat down or police harassment, receive the same level of courtesy, you need to do more than your white peers on all levels. This is just what you need to do. Even then there is no guarantee. And, no, it is definitely not fair."

Now, in no way is our situation nearly the same as the heartbreaking struggles that African Americans have had to put up with for hundreds of years. The comparison is not even close.

I simply wish to draw on the analogy that we, as atheists, agnostics and free thinkers within Alcoholics Anonymous, a christian organization in denial of the fact that it is a christian organization, should be model citizens in order to make secular recovery attractive to those who might be swayed as much by our behavior as by our words.

I know, every group has its eccentrics, and our cause may come close to having a corner on that market. But I want to put in a pitch for salesmanship, for making secular recovery look good.

I am not arguing that we should behave in a conformist manner, but rather that we have a special obligation to walk the talk, to be living examples of sobriety, in every sense of the word. WE should be that serene member who is content to be sober; whole and complete without any gods; not on the defensive; with no axe to grind; and not looking to get up on a soapbox and hide our insecurity behind an anti-theist rant. Sure we are going to suffer pain and setbacks in sobriety. But even then we can be walking, talking examples of the graceful, sustainable application of the core principles of recovery.

Most of our AA friends are going to be far more forgiving and accepting of us than we generally are of ourselves. We are often our own worst enemies. As usually is the case in life, most of the really scary stuff happens in between our ears.

But remember, for everyone who turns a cold shoulder your way, there are silent ones thanking you, either now or in the future. You are making it safer and easier for others. There may be a dozen people, new, old, or somewhere in between, who never realized that coming out was an option, people who will silently, unbeknownst to you, draw courage from your courage, strength from your strength.

I think it is important to speak in the first person. That is, and I think this is very important: do not berate or attack the beliefs of others. Word your thoughts carefully, because I think we do the secularization movement more harm than good if we antagonize, criticize, or make theistic traditionalists defensive.

Don't talk down spirituality. Talk up secularism.

Demonstrate through word and deed your genuine respect for their beliefs. Read about the history of Alcoholics Anonymous. Remember all the good that AA, coming from the historic roots in which it was born, has brought to us. Remember all the good within everyone around you. Show that respect in your words. They will be filled with self-righteous anger and defensiveness if they feel attacked by argumentative, critical atheists. But if they are surrounded by serene, soft-spoken atheists who practice what they preach, well, we will probably catch a lot more flies with that honey.

Learn. That is something I am doing.

Learn more about our shared history, and that knowledge will inform your speech. Talk about what you learn, at group level or with individuals. Learn about our history, and make your shares well-informed and knowledgeable. Knowledge is power. Along these lines, in addition to resources mentioned earlier, try:

- *Not-God: A History of Alcoholics Anonymous*. By Ernie Kurtz

- *Don't Tell: Stories and Essays by Agnostics and Atheists in AA*. Edited by Roger C. (anthology)

And, not exactly on recovery per se, but related:

- *Coming Out Atheist: How to do It, How to Help Each Other, and Why*. By Greta Christina

- *The Portable Atheist*. By Christopher Hitchens (anthology)

Inform people about Jimmy Burwell's revolutionary importance, the history of agnostic groups, the currently expanding secular meeting movement, about some of Bill's commentary in support of the third tradition, his occasional, outspoken, sense of regret at allowing the whole thing to "shift" so far to the religious side. Help people place AA's birth within the historical context of old-time religion and faith healing. Help them make the shift to current times, with the growth of secularism and the incredible growth of knowledge in the areas of behavioral, cognitive, and neural sciences.

Find the common ground. This is what I have been writing about for many pages, so I will not elaborate any further. But, in many cases, we and our theistic brethren are actually talking about the same thing, or at least something very similar. Find common ground with your "opponent". I greatly enjoyed a couple of conversations with Reverend Ward Ewing during the convention on just this topic. Ultimately, there are real and irreconcilable differences between theists and atheists, of course. But this may not be the time to focus on such issues. For the moment, it may be more advisable to focus on our primary purpose: staying sober and helping other alcoholics achieve sobriety.

I think it is important to stress the value of practicing what you preach, of being the change you want to see. If you spout the third tradition, you need to apply it across the board. Are there dirty street people sucking up the free coffee and doughnuts at your meeting? Talk to them if you can. What if we completely disagree with what one person has to say, are you still willing to go to bat for her or his right to say it? It doesn't just have to be about our favored WAAFT related causes. Individual's rights to have unpopular opinions should be sacrosanct and vehemently guarded, whether we like them or not. This furthermore marks us as the kind of members who safeguard the principles, above and beyond their "personal" applications to our preferred positions.

Stay off the pulpit. Do not preach. Prove the program works (even without the god part), through simple shares about daily life. Sprinkle in a sentence or two about the role of your secular belief, practice or interpretation, or just leave it implied. But do not belabor the point. Remain humble and quiet about it. A properly placed sentence in an appropriate context does wonders, while speeches just turn people off.

Here is, in my opinion, the easiest thing you can do if you really do not want to rock the boat. Just sit silently through any parts that mention god or whatever religious word you don't like. Refuse to participate. Take a page from quiet inaction. I know a fair number of us choose this course of action, such as abstaining from *The Lord's Prayer*. So the Gandhi/King path of peaceful inaction is another approach in our arsenal of tools. Although it does feel kinda weird to say Gandhi, King and arsenal in the same sentence…

I took a slightly more proactive page from that school the other day. The secretary asked me if I'd read the fifth chapter section, which most of us know. Begins with "Rarely have we seen a person fail who has thoroughly followed our path" and ends with "God could and would if he were sought". In the middle there are over a dozen references to divine intervention and faith healing and I just can't read that stuff with a straight face anymore.

I was sorely tempted to read it and make some humorous, sarcastic adjustments along the way. But my better half took control and I said to the secretary, in a very kindly tone, "I'm sorry. I can't read that. There are to many parts I just disagree with". And that was the end of it. I spent the next fifteen minutes wondering if that did any good. I decided in favor of the butterfly's wings: every little action counts and, in the end, they will hopefully add up to noticeable change.

Always remain non-confrontational, yet never be afraid to enter into conversations. If you are a role model of "god-less" recovery, people are eventually going to start asking you questions. Just mention it casually during your average share.

Someone will come up to you and ask you how you do it. Answer frankly and honestly. And then, hopefully, the whole thing starts to spread, slowly but surely.

Now, to move towards the slightly more confrontational, here is something I sometimes do, and especially when people say something along the "spiritual not religious" line. I ask people to clarify their terms. When people use vague or religious language, especially when they utter "deepities" (see Dennett or Boghossian) I will sometimes ask them after the meeting to clarify what they mean. Seek humanistic, secular clarity. Force them to speak a language you can understand. Force them, through simple Socratic inquiry, to clarify what they mean when they say "higher power", "spirit", or "spirituality". This need not be done in an antagonistic manner. I do this, and I do it respectfully, letting them know that, quite honestly, I literally do not know what they mean.

Another slightly more aggressive move is to advocate for approved readings that do not refer to god, spirit, or anything supernatural. These can be found within Conference-approved literature. But groups are allowed, if the group conscience agrees, to use non-approved literature as well.

So start a movement. Yeah, I know that sounds big. But it really isn't. It can start very small and easy. Start talking to one or two like-minded friends at a favored meeting. See if you can get a core group together to agree on specific changes to the opening or closing routines that make them less religious. Get your little revolutionary cadre to populate the next business meeting and offer up a suggestion. We can try and get individual meetings to change their opening and closing traditions, taking the god out of them, by a simple vote following a simple campaign.

Go to business meetings. We can't complain about nothing changing if we haven't gone to the business meeting and brought up some options, raised some consciousness, and caused a few people to start thinking about these ideas. Make reasonable proposals, for example that only agnostic-friendly readings be sanctioned for group usage in accordance with the third tradition. Advocate for the cause in a non-confrontation manner. Quote Bill Wilson at them: "God as I understood Him had to be for everybody. Sometimes my aggression was subtle and sometimes it was crude. But either way it was damaging – perhaps fatally so – to numbers of non-believers."

Become a group secretary. Of course a secretary does not have much power at all per se. But, as a secretary you may have some choice over who your speakers are, over which readings are being read, about what literature is placed on the literature table, and even over the range of topics. You may have the opportunity to insert atheist, agnostic, and free-thinking speakers, readings, recitations, and topics into the group discourse that might otherwise not be there.

Going even further up the food chain, volunteering to become a GSR or a representative in general service might put you in a position to advocate even more effectively for our cause. Hell, I don't even know what they do. But you can bet such positions will give you multiple opportunities to further secular recovery perspectives. At the very least you will have the opportunity to bring up topics and bring them to the forefront of conversations and people's consciousness.

I am almost out of ideas, thank god. But I do think this one is very important: use your personal gifts. Some of us are good at public speaking, dazzling the gang at our local AA meeting with our sparkling wit and gift for gab. Use it. Others sponsor by the dozens. Do what you do well in the name of the cause.

Use your gifts. I like to write. Maybe you are a painter. Maybe you are a party organizer. Maybe you are a musician who can play at a party. Maybe you are a business organizer. Use your skills to advocate for the cause.

But always keep in mind that we are really on the same page, really all after the same thing. You catch more flies with honey. Be non-confrontational. These people are our heritage. Without them and their religion we might not even be alive today. Think of the religious members as kind, giving, and compassionate, often wise founders, if somewhat outdated. We can add to their knowledge without attacking them or wounding their pride.

It's maybe just getting near time to leave the old ferry, sitting on the shore, no longer needed, take the parts we do need, and walk away onward on our path forward, remembering it fondly.

Nothing to Fear

All my life I have known fear. Fear and I, we go way back. But there is a specific kind of fear I remember feeling back in the late 1980s.

I had more or less just settled into sober living, a new thing to me. I had also settled in to a family, with a beautiful young wife I loved dearly, and a brand new amazing baby daughter. I had escaped New York City just as my friends and cohorts started losing limbs to heroin and getting stabbed to death over LSD deals gone awry. In a highly poignant juxtaposition, like the cover of a Crosby, Stills & Nash album or a highly ironic Norman Rockwell painting, I had found myself living in a cozy wooden shack with a sweet wife, cute kitchen, claw foot tub to bathe the giggling baby in, apple trees, and a kitty cat named Sara all in an old orchard surrounded by Redwoods. A whole new life for me, one I never thought I would have. The Roxas Men's group had become my home group, on Roxas Street in Santa Cruz, California. It was like I had died and gone to heaven.

But controversy, as always, reared its ugly head. The old men in the group squabbled endlessly with the middle-aged and especially the younger ones. What was the issue? Whether or not it was ok to talk about drugs other than alcohol in our Alcoholics Anonymous meetings. That was the issue at the time. Some of you remember the endless point/counter-point. I will spare you the rehash. Each side had very valid points to make. But, many of us feared the controversy would tear AA asunder.

I had opinions. They would change with every good argument I heard. What did "Black" Henry think? "Fireman" John? John Grey? "Spiritual" Ed Brown, my sponsor for years? I looked up to these guys. What did they think? Some of them seemed nervous, and frightened, like this controversy could really tear our good thing apart. And so I knew a new fear. Fresh from dealing drugs on the streets of New York, here I was, frightened that my beloved little life boat of AA might be capsized because this controversy was too much for it to bear.

One day it occurred to me in a moment of insight that Alcoholics Anonymous would be just fine. Time would find an answer, and people's needs would get met. At least where I live, this old topic is very rarely one which upsets anyone anymore. In fact it is the source of a couple of real old, inside jokes. But very few, if any, members are afraid of Alcoholics Anonymous dying as a result of this once-raging controversy.

Alcoholics Anonymous is a Christian organization that is pretending not to be a Christian organization, but it has developed a wealth of other "tools" which are now a part of its toolkit. So, those of us that are disinterested in supernatural beliefs and faith-healing, yet still wish to remain in the tribe and be welcome, we want it to be recognized that, simply because one of the many available tools does not work for us, that does not mean *we* do not belong. We very much do belong. We belong because AA's traditions themselves tell us that:

> *Alcoholics Anonymous membership ought never depend upon conformity. The only requirement for membership is a desire to stop drinking. Our membership ought to include all who suffer from alcoholism. We refuse none who wish to recover.*

Secular AA Online Resources

AA Agnostica (aaagnostica.org)

AA Agnostica is a website.

AA Agnostica is a publisher.

AA Agnostica is a space for AA agnostics, atheists and freethinkers worldwide.

In all of those roles, AA Agnostica attempts to be a helping hand for the alcoholic who reaches out to Alcoholics Anonymous for help and finds that she or he is disturbed by the religious content of many AA meetings.

AA Agnostica is not affiliated with any group in AA or any other organization. Contributors to the AA Agnostica website – or to our books – are all members of Alcoholics Anonymous, unless otherwise indicated. The views they express are neither their groups' nor those of AA, but solely their own.

There are an increasing number of groups within AA that are not religious in their thinking or practice. These groups don't recite prayers at the beginning or ending of their meetings, nor do they suggest that a belief in God is required to get sober or to maintain sobriety. If the readings at their meetings include AA's suggested program of recovery, then a secular or humanist version of the 12 Steps is shared.

If you asked members of AA who belong to these nonreligious groups about their vision of the fellowship, they would probably describe it this way:

> *Alcoholics Anonymous is a fellowship of men and women who share their experience, strength and hope with*

each other that they may solve their common problem and help others recover from alcoholism. The only requirement for AA membership is a desire to stop drinking. There are no dues or fees for membership: we are self-supporting through our own contributions. AA is not allied with any sect, denomination, politics, organization or institution: neither endorses nor opposes any causes. Our primary purpose is to stay sober and help other alcoholics to achieve sobriety.

AA Agnostica does not endorse or oppose any form of religion or atheism. Our only wish is to ensure suffering alcoholics that they can find sobriety in AA without having to accept anyone else's beliefs or having to deny their own.

The word "Agnostica" is derived from Chapter Four, "We Agnostics," of Alcoholics Anonymous, otherwise known as the "Big Book". When we use the word "agnostic" in relation to AA – or words like "atheist" or "freethinker" – we are simply referring to the specific wisdom of groups and individuals within the fellowship who understand that a belief in "God" is not necessary for recovery from alcoholism. It is the experience, strength and hope of these women and men which form the basis for the pages and posts on the AA Agnostica website and its published works and which are meant to be a comfort and an inspiration for others in AA.

AA Beyond Belief (aabeyondbelief.org)

AA Beyond Belief is a website and podcast, but it's much more than that. AA Beyond Belief is a refuge, a home in AA for agnostics, atheists, freethinkers, and all others who seek a secular path of recovery within Alcoholics Anonymous.

At AA Beyond Belief you can participate in a global fellowship of secular members of AA. Here you will find personal recovery stories of agnostics and atheists expressed through blog posts, audio recordings, poetry, and video. You will also find articles about AA history, the Steps and Traditions, book reviews, and the latest in the science of addiction.

The content at AA Beyond Belief is created by our community, so we welcome and encourage you to use this site as a platform for sharing your experience, strength, and hope as a secular person in AA. Please send your personal stories whether in written form or in audio/video format. Submit your poetry, your photography, your artwork. Any medium can be used to communicate recovery, and it's all welcomed at AA Beyond Belief.

The AA Beyond Belief Podcast was started in September 2015, and it has been well received by the recovery community. The podcast features personal stories, and interviews with authors and experts in addiction medicine. The podcast also covers the Steps, Traditions, and even looks at other recovery options outside of AA. If you would like to appear on the podcast, please drop us a line. We would love to talk with you.

Contact AA Beyond Belief by sending an email to editor@aabeyondbelief.org

Printed in Great Britain
by Amazon